A R T *of* DARKNESS

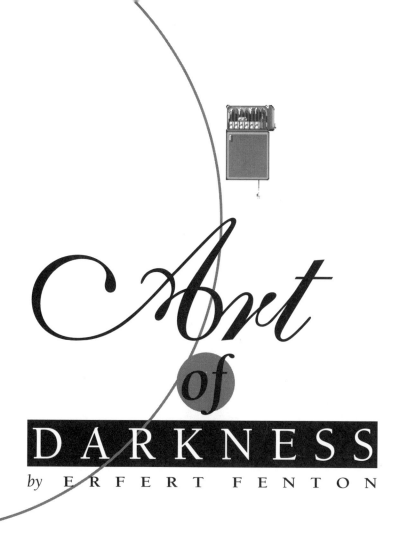

Art of

DARKNESS

by ERFERT FENTON

PEACHPIT PRESS

ART OF DARKNESS
Erfert Fenton

PEACHPIT PRESS, INC.
2414 Sixth St.
Berkeley, CA 94710
(510) 548-4393
(510) 548-5991 (fax)

Copyright © 1992 by Erfert Fenton
Cover design by Ted Mader & Associates (TMA)
Cover illustration by Robert Dietz, TMA
Interior design by Olav Martin Kvern
Color plates by Venkatesh

The text of this book is set in Adobe Systems' ITC Berkeley Oldstyle; chapter titles are set in Bitstream's Shelley Allegro and Shelley Volante.

ISBN 1-56609-012-1
0 9 8 7 6 5 4 3 2 1

Printed and bound in the United States of America

Contents

Acknowledgments

I'd like to thank the following people for their assistance: Cathy Abes, Scott Armitage, Dann Auld, Patrick Beard, Gregory Becker, Joan Blades, Wes Boyd, Inam Choudhary, Jack Eastman, Jay Fenton, Ed Fries, Ed Hall, Ben Haller, Andy Karn, Olav Kvern, Jenny Lens, Brian Lowry, Ma and Pa, Daman Mahal, Mark Malamud, Ted Nace, Felicity O'Meara, Lon Poole, Nick Rush, Tom Saxton, Mike Schutte, Jean Tantra, Levi Thomas, Peter Van Vorous, Rob Vaterlaus, and Larry Yaeger. Thanks also to the rest of the gang at Berkeley Systems.

I'm especially grateful to Bruce Burkhalter, who helped coordinate this project even though he had other fish to fry (and toasters to fly).

— Erfert Fenton
1992

Introduction

The first thing you see when you walk into Berkeley Systems is a huge aquarium filled with brightly colored tropical fish. If you head past the lobby and into the conference room, you'll come across their extensive collection of toasters (terrestrial toasters all, except for the Berkeley Systems mascot, an actual General Electric Toastmaster with metal wings grafted on).

Things were not always so plush at Berkeley Systems. Not so many years ago, the company's employees toiled in a tiny garret. Eight or nine people crammed themselves into the attic of an old Victorian house in Berkeley; to reach the office, one had to climb a set of stairs that resembled a ladder.

But Berkeley Systems has come quite a way since those humble beginnings, thanks largely to the success of a product they originally offered not because they thought it would be incredibly successful, but because they thought it was neat.

Early in 1989, Berkeley Systems' main product was Stepping Out, a Macintosh program that provided the software equivalent of a large monitor. The company's programmers were also working on software for computer users with disabilities. Their inLARGE program magnified the contents of the screen to assist partially-sighted computer users, while outSPOKEN gave the Mac an audible interface for blind users.

One day, Berkeley Systems programmer Patrick Beard brought in a disk that held a program his friend Jack Eastman had written. It was a modular screen saver that let users plug different displays into a core program. Berkeley Systems founders Wes Boyd and Joan Blades liked the program, and decided to take a stab at marketing it. Screen savers themselves were not a new concept at the time, but nobody had released anything that worked quite like Jack's modular application.

Jack, Patrick, and a few other Berkeley Systems programmers set to work on refining Jack's original program. They came up with the 15 modules that were to become After Dark 1.0. (The product was originally going to be called Night Life, but that name was already taken, so they came up with After Dark.)

The program made its debut at the Macworld Expo in August 1989. Its introduction was not exactly a splash. Berkeley Systems didn't have a booth, but instead rented a small corner of a mail-order company's huge booth, placing two employees and a Mac on duty. None of the trade show attendees knew who these people were, or why they were displaying things like munching worms and falling raindrops on their Mac, but once people realized they were looking at a set of adjustable screen savers, the response was generally favorable.

Little by little, After Dark caught on. According to Nick Rush, now Berkeley Systems' executive vice president, "In the early days, nobody had any idea how big a product it would be. Our main concern was whether we could make enough to support the cost of the packaging." But they knew they were onto something. At Nick's urging, high-quality graphics and sound were added to After Dark, more modules were added, and After Dark 2.0 made its debut at the August 1990 Macworld Expo. Thanks to eye-catching modules such as Flying Toasters and Fish!, the program was a huge success.

Berkeley Systems held an After Dark module programming contest in 1990, and several of the contest winners — as well as some new modules by Berkeley Systems programmers — were released in 1991 as More After Dark. The company had a second contest in 1992, which resulted in a flood of entries.

Stay tuned for another batch of great modules, including some of the 1992 contest winners, sometime in the future.

So why a book about After Dark? Well, why not? After all, After Dark probably shows up on your screen more than any other program you own. If you step away from your desk for a few minutes, chances are your screen will be filled with flying toasters, swimming sea-life, or some such silliness when you return. You don't see spreadsheets or word processors popping up on their own every five minutes (at least I hope you don't), and yet you spend plenty of time learning how to use these programs to their best advantage. So why not learn to get more out of your After Dark modules? You could add an octopus to your Fish! module, perhaps, or put a pat of butter on your flying toast. With the knowledge you'll gain from this book, After Dark could become a new form of self-expression, a vehicle for computer folk art, a stimulating hobby, or perhaps the key to living the full and meaningful life you've always dreamed of. Who am I kidding? It's just a bunch of screen savers. But this book could help you have a little fun with them.

Chapter 1 presents an introduction to screen savers and describes the basic workings of After Dark. Chapter 2 describes each module in After Dark and More After Dark, as well as the ten new modules on the disk that accompanies this book. Chapter 3 shows you how to combine After Dark modules into custom MultiModules and offers numerous recipes for same. Chapter 4 offers advanced tips for customizing various After Dark modules. The Resources section tells you where to find many of the programs and services mentioned in the book.

Screen Salvation Basics

After Dark

CHAPTER 1

Screen Salvation Basics

What Is a Screen Saver?

After Dark is a set of *screen savers,* displays designed to keep your Mac's screen from being damaged when it's left on for long periods. How could your screen get damaged? Well, it's like this. The inside surface of the Mac's screen is coated with phosphor, a substance that emits light when excited. Inside the monitor is a little electron gun (or a battalion of three guns if you have a color monitor) that sweeps back and forth across the inside of the screen, zapping the appropriate pixels (dots) on the screen as instructed by software. The electron gun zips across each line of the screen, moving from top to bottom in about $1/60$ of a second. This screen setup, which consists of a series of horizontal lines, is called a *raster* display, from the Latin word for rake. (Don't worry, there will not be a quiz at the end of this chapter.) By the time the beam reaches the bottom of the screen, the phosphor at the top is starting to lose its glow; fortunately, your eyes can't process information that quickly, and you don't notice a thing as the electron gun hightails it to the top of the screen and begins scanning again.

With all that scanning and beaming, the screen's phosphor coating takes quite a beating. As a result, if the same image is displayed for a long time, it can create a ghost image in the phosphor, a phenomenon known as screen burn-in. You may

Fun with Science Tip #1: If you peer closely at your Mac's monitor, you'll see that the display is made up of hundreds of tiny horizontal lines. That's nice. But if you really want to have fun, stand several feet away from your screen and look at it while chewing something crunchy, such as hard candy or granola.

not leave your Mac on all the time, but chances are it sits idle for some time each day as you make phone calls, attend meetings, or hang around the water cooler. A screen saver like After Dark saves the day by kicking in with an ever-changing image after a specified amount of time, which prevents the phosphor in any particular part of the screen from becoming overexcited.

Let's face it, screen burn-in may not be right at the top of your list of worries, but it never hurts to take good care of your investments. Besides, After Dark's modules take care of a problem that's just as damaging — if not more so — than screen burn-in: brain burn-out. Numerous studies involving assorted bored primates have shown that animals (including you, dear reader) have a need for *stimulus variation,* known in layman's terms as something interesting going on. After Dark's modules certainly fill that requirement, offering a variety of absorbing patterns, sounds, animations, and even games.

A screen saver doesn't *have* to be interesting; it could simply black out the screen after a set amount of time, but that's no fun. The folks at Berkeley Systems figured they could do better than that. Of course, some people just don't wanna have fun, as illustrated by the following exchange.

In late 1989, Berkeley Systems sent out a mailing that offered After Dark for 40% off the regular price. The offer said, in part, "Even if you already have a screen saver, you'll still want After Dark, because After Dark does much more than just blank your screen...." Nick Rush, executive vice president of Berkeley Systems, received the original offer letter back, with a terse note scrawled on it by a Mr. X (not his real name). Mr. X insisted that he didn't want to do anything more than blank his screen. He didn't believe the nonsense about needing to be reminded that one's computer was running, and demanded to know why a simple screen blanker wasn't one of After Dark's built-in options.

Nick replied:

January 11, 1990

Dear Mr. X:

Thank you for your communication regarding our 40% off offer on After Dark. We are always pleased to hear the opinions of our valued Berkeley Systems customers.

In your remarks, you indicated that you didn't want to do more than blank your screen, and asked why that wasn't one of the built-in options. I'm happy to report that it is. After Dark includes a module called Fade Away that blacks out the screen when it engages, either suddenly or incrementally depending on your settings.

Now it's true that if you only want your screen saved you can acquire less complicated software that will do the job. But people want more. Why do people have a closet full of different clothes when the same dull uniform day after day would suffice? Why do people go out for nice dinners when a bowl of gruel and a handful of dietary supplements would adequately sustain them? Because they enjoy it. People like variety and they like being entertained. And After Dark is loaded with both. Certainly every product is not for everyone, and you're entitled to your opinion, but if you gave it a chance, *you* might like it, too.

In fact, I'm willing to send you After Dark for *50%* off. And not just regular After Dark. I'll send you the as yet unreleased, new and improved After Dark version 1.1, with smoother animation and three new modules. All for a mere twenty dollars. I'll even throw in the postage. Send me a check made out to Berkeley Systems for twenty dollars, and I'll personally mail you After Dark 1.1. I'm confident, Mr. X, that you'll like it.

I look forward to hearing from you.

Sincerely,

Nicholas Rush

Nicholas Rush
Berkeley Systems, Inc.

Mr. X grudgingly sent his check for $20 to purchase After Dark, along with Nick's letter of January 11, again with a note written on it. In this note, Mr. X opined that while some people might want more, he wasn't one of them. And furthermore, he suspected that many of the people in his office shared his opinions on screen savers, and didn't want to be distracted by dynamic screen displays while they were trying to work. He repeated his request for a no-nonsense screen blanker.

Mr. X's order was filled and his check cashed. Nick wrote a personal note on the invoice, saying "Thank you for your order — I'm sure you'll enjoy it." But two weeks later, Mr. X returned his copy of After Dark, this time with a message on the returned invoice. He was very disappointed that Fade Away did not make his screen go absolutely black. Because of this flaw, he found it unacceptable and asked for his money back. He expressed his utter amazement that Berkeley Systems persisted in being so stubborn in this matter.

Mr. X was right; even when set to 0% intensity, Fade Away leaves a barely perceptible glow on the screen. So, a refund check was promptly sent, along with not only another personal note from Nick, but a gift as well.

February 5, 1990

Dear Mr. X:

I'm sorry you were dissatisfied with our product, After Dark. Your refund check is enclosed. I have also returned the copy of After Dark you purchased, modified to operate precisely to your specifications. When you reinstall After Dark, you will discover only two modules to select from in the Control Panel: Starry Night and one called Mr. X. Mr. X has no controls. When it engages, your screen will go instantly and totally black. Unfortunately I could not remove the Starry Night module, as it is built into the program.

This is a gift, Mr. X, in consideration for all your time and trouble. Honestly, we're not trying to be stubborn; we just want you, and everyone who deals with our company, to be happy.

Sincerely,

Nicholas Rush

Nicholas Rush
Berkeley Systems, Inc.

Once again, Mr. X returned Nick's letter, again with a note scrawled across it. This one stated that he found the latest disk satisfactory, and that he was returning Nick's refund check.

Another satisfied customer! I think it's safe to say that Mr. X does not represent the typical After Dark user. Contrary to Mr. X's belief, many people actually enjoy having a dynamic screen display that can be relaxing, beautiful, entertaining, humorous, or even absurd. But many After Dark owners aren't getting nearly as much enjoyment out of After Dark as they could, if they'd just take ten or fifteen minutes to experiment.

The principal purpose of this book is to nudge people into having more fun with After Dark. (Well, that's not quite true. The principal purpose of this book, as far as I'm concerned, is to make me lots of money so I can summer in the South of France [someday I hope to be wealthy enough to use *summer* as a verb]…but I'd be very happy if the book helped bring some chortles to the cubicles of Corporate America.) Depending on how much effort you want to invest, this book might prompt you to simply fiddle with the settings of your favorite module, discover an existing module you'd overlooked, find new modules on an electronic bulletin board, create a MultiModule masterpiece, or even customize a module or two with a resource editor.

In case you're a newcomer to After Dark, let's start with some basic information.

Installation

Frankly, I'm not going to go into much detail in this section. Installing After Dark is right near the top of the easiness scale.

To install the After Dark program, simply drag the After Dark icon and the After Dark Files folder into the System folder. If you're running System 6, that's all there is to it. If you're running System 7, you have a choice of installation procedures. You can drag the After Dark icon and the After

Turned on, burned
in, bummed out.
— Anon.

Dark Files folder into the System folder (make sure the System folder is closed before you drag the files into it). A dialog box will ask you if you'd like to have After Dark automatically placed in the Control Panels folder, where it belongs. Sure, why not? Click OK and the After Dark icon will be placed in the Control Panels folder. Or, you can open the System folder and install both components. Drag the After Dark Files folder into the System folder itself, and the After Dark icon into the Control Panels folder that resides in the System folder.

After Dark won't show up immediately after you install it. You must restart your Mac to complete the installation procedure.

The first time you open After Dark, a registration dialog box will appear. Type your name and company name, then click OK.

To install More After Dark, simply insert the More After Dark disk, double-click the Installer icon, and select the After Dark Files folder as the destination folder. Click the Extract button, and the More After Dark modules will be placed in the After Dark Files folder. *Note: You must have After Dark installed in order to run the More After Dark modules.*

More After Dark also includes After Dark Updater, a utility that automatically updates your version of After Dark if necessary. (After Dark version 2.0u or later is required to run the More After Dark modules; this version also provides full System 7 compatibility.) *Note: The After Dark Updater is also included on the disk that accompanies this book.* If you have an older version of After Dark, double-click the After Dark Updater icon to run the updater.

Tip: To see which version of After Dark you have, open After Dark (see the following section if you need instructions for accessing After Dark) and click the After Dark logo in the upper left-hand corner of the After Dark window. The version number will then appear in the upper right-hand corner of the window.

After Dark Essentials

After Dark is a Control Panel device (or *cdev*, if you really want to impress people with what a techno-weenie you are). Under System 6, you open After Dark by choosing Control Panel from the Apple menu, then clicking the After Dark icon in the window that appears. Under System 7, After Dark resides in the Control Panels folder. You can open After Dark by opening the System folder, then opening the Control Panels folder, then double-clicking the After Dark icon. For faster access under System 7, choose Control Panels from the Apple menu to immediately enter the Control Panels folder. For the quickest access of all (under System 7), you can make an alias of the After Dark icon and place it in a convenient spot, such as the desktop. To make an alias, simply click the After Dark icon to select it, then choose Make Alias from the File menu.

When you open After Dark, you'll see this:

All installed modules are listed on the left. Scroll to the module you want, then click on it to select it (or type the first few letters of its name for even quicker access).

Click the Off button to disable After Dark at any time. The When button allows you to set how long the Mac must be idle before After Dark comes on, as well as several other factors.

You can set a *sleep corner,* a corner of the screen where you can place the pointer to activate After Dark. You can also specify a *never sleep corner;* placing the pointer in that corner prevents After Dark from engaging.

Checking the SystemIQ Monitor option prevents After Dark from engaging if the Mac is busy with other processes, such as printing or telecommunications. SystemIQ checks acitivity on your Mac's hard disk, as well as its printer and modem ports. If SystemIQ determines that the Mac is busy, it won't allow After Dark to display until the Mac is free. If After Dark is already running when SystemIQ indicates that the Mac is busy, After Dark's animation will slow down to give more processing time to the Mac.

When you click on a module name in the After Dark control panel, a set of controls for that module appears. Controls generally consist of pop-up menus and sliders that let you control everything from Number of Cats to Twanginess. Some modules also let you adjust their sound level.

Click the triangle in the bottom right-hand corner to see more information about the selected module.

Screen Savers and PowerBooks

A note to PowerBook users: Apple's PowerBooks use a liquid-crystal display (LCD) instead of a phosphor-coated monitor. Although an LCD could experience a type of image burn-in, it's not likely to occur, mainly because most PowerBook users aren't likely to keep their machines running for long periods (unless they have extensive battery collections or habitually power their PowerBooks from a wall outlet). Therefore, a

11

screen saver isn't really necessary (unless, of course, you have a burning need to play Lunatic Fringe). A more practical solution is to turn down the PowerBook's backlight when you're not using it. To automate the backlight-dimming process, you can use a utility like BackLight Control, a cdev that dims the PowerBook's backlight during periods of in-activity. BackLight Control can be found on online services such as CompuServe.

Now that you know the basics, let's move on to the specifics. The following chapter provides information on dozens of After Dark modules.

Modules On Parade

Modules On Parade

This chapter describes each module in the original After Dark package, each one in the More After Dark sequel, and the ten modules on the disk that accompanies this book. In addition, a selection of public-domain and shareware modules are described in the final section of the chapter. The descriptions are intended to augment the program's skimpy manual, provide tips where appropriate, and generally encourage you to explore some of the modules.

After Dark Modules

This section describes the 31 modules that are included with the After Dark package.

Bouncing Ball

Bouncing Ball is not one of your more exciting After Dark modules, but that's OK — it's not supposed to be. This module is provided as a sample for programmers who want to write After Dark modules. (You may have noticed a Programming Examples folder on your After Dark disk, as well as a programming section in the manual.)

But even nonprogrammers can have a litttle fun with Bouncing Ball. It may be minimalist, but it offers a lot of variety. For the starkest screen saver ever, set both the ball's size and speed to 0. The result is a stationary white dot. Think of it as a scathing, neo-nihilistic statement on the relationship between carbon-based life-forms and silicon-based thinking machines. Or, if you're of a more frenetic bent, you can really annoy anyone who passes your computer if you set the speed to 100, the ball size to 5 or so, and the volume to maximum. This combo is virtually guaranteed to induce a case of the screaming meemies within ten minutes.

Can of Worms

In Can of Worms, by Jack Eastman, a gang of worms consumes whatever's on the screen, complete with a disconcerting crunching sound. (The worm-chomping sound effect was created, in part, by several members of the Berkeley Systems staff hunkered around a microphone, chewing on crackers, celery, and other crunchy foodstuffs. Also mixed into the brew is the sound of Executive VP Nick Rush's infant daughter chewing on a biscuit. What a sentimental guy!)

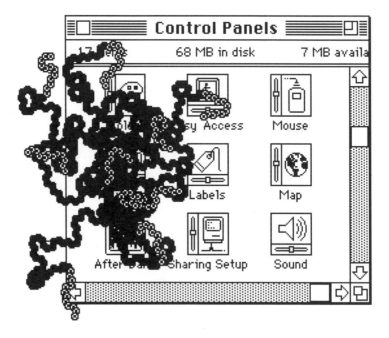

You can set the number of worms (1 to 20), segments per worm (2 to 20), and degree of wiggliness (0 to 100). Note Berkeley Systems' attention to detail; a less exacting software company might have offered from 1 to 20 segments per worm, but a one-segment worm wouldn't be a true worm at all (that is, a member of the group of worms called *annelids,* a group that includes our friend the earthworm), but rather some sort of slug (a terrestrial pulmonate gastropod known for its un-hurried demeanor). This is just the first example that proves that After Dark is not just a set of screen savers, but a valuable educational aid as well.

Clock

Clock, by Rob Vaterlaus, is a practical sort of screen saver, since it displays a clock that actually tells time. You can choose from among several clocks: three analog models (one antique and two modern), and a digital display. The digital clock also offers a fancy option wherein the digits representing seconds blend into one another.

If the Clock module doesn't display the correct time, you can reset the clock in the Mac's General control panel. In System 6, choose Control Panel from the Apple menu, then click the General icon. In System 7, select Control Panels from the Apple menu, then double-click on the General Controls icon in the folder that appears. Set the Mac's clock to the right time in the control panel that appears.

Doodles

If you work in one of those paperless offices one keeps hearing about, you undoubtedly miss doodling on a piece of scratch paper while you're talking on the phone. Well, your troubles are over, thanks to After Dark. Now your computer can do your doodling for you with Jack Eastman's Doodles module.

Doodles offers several controls. Use the Number pop-up menu to set columns and rows of doodles (the 4 × 3 setting, for example, gives you four doodles across and three down). The Granularity slider adjusts the smoothness of the doodles' curves, from 15 (jagged) to 180 (smooth). The Complexity slider specifies how complicated the doodles are, from 1 (simple) to 7 (scribbly). The Walk slider lets you set how scrunched up or stretched out (to use the technical terminology) the doodles are. A setting of 0 produces tight, squiggly doodles, while 100 creates wide, simple shapes reminiscent of graphs or waveforms.

If you set Number to 4×3, Granularity to 180, Complexity to 7, and Walk to around 60, you'll swear that your Mac is writing you messages.

Down the Drain

Remember when you first learned about the Coriolis effect (named after the French civil engineer Gaspard G. Coriolis, I'm sure you'll recall), a deflecting force caused by the earth's rotation? You learned that, thanks to this effect, water flows down the drain in a counterclockwise direction in the Northern hemisphere, and in a clockwise direction in the Southern hemisphere. Then, there was that inevitable moment when you wondered, "Gee, what happens to water at the equator? If you draw a bath, are you just stuck with the same water forever, since the clockwise and counterclockwise forces would exactly balance each other? How do the people who live there bathe and brush their teeth?"

Programmer Rob Vaterlaus answers those very questions with his educational module Down the Drain, which slurps the contents of your screen into a drain. Sliders let you set the drainage speed (from Slow to Fast) and direction (Clockwise so After Dark users in the Southern hemisphere won't feel disoriented, Counterclockwise for Northerners, and Inward for those of you who reside on the equator). Having never been to the equator, I'm not positive that water slides straight down the drain at the equator, but it's as good a theory as any.

I asked my local reference librarian what happened at the equator, drainagewise, but I'm afraid she was stumped. In fact, she seemed a bit peeved when she called me back. She said, "You know, I suspect that the people who wrote scientific reports on the Coriolis force never suspected anyone would *care* how water went down the drain at the equator." Can't argue with her there.)

Fade Away

Fade Away, by Jack Eastman, is a simple screen saver (it merely dims the screen to whatever brightness level you specify), but one that can offer deep psychological insights when you carefully observe a subject using it. Refer to Chapter 1 for an example of one personality type — someone so pragmatic he actually wanted Fade Away to fade even further than its current settings. A more flamboyant person might use Fade Away to more dramatic ends: "Ma! Everything's goin' dark. Where are you, Ma? I can't see you...." Myself, I like to set the Intensity level to 100%, creating an anti-screen-saver that doesn't do anything at all! What does that say about my personality? Go figure.

Fish!

Fish! is probably the most popular After Dark module of them all. It's based on an earlier program by Ed Fries and Tom Saxton, the principals of Tom & Ed's Bogus Software. Some of you oldtimers out there might remember Ed and Tom's original Fish program, which was not a screen saver but a utility that simply placed a variety of swimming sea creatures on the Mac's desktop.

Fish! started out as a Macintosh programming exercise, since Ed Fries traditionally liked to write a fish display to try out a new programming environment. Some of his earliest fish — which were created back in the days when computers were huge, clunky contraptions that accepted input via punch cards

from the pocket-protector set — were made up entirely of displayed numbers and letters, since graphics programs as we now know them didn't exist. Tom saw one of Ed's fish programs one day, and volunteered his services as a co-programmer. The Mac version improved upon the alpha-numeric fish, offering color graphics of cartoon-like fish, mermaids, other sea creatures, and even a hapless fellow named "Sinkin' Jimmy," who descended the screen sporting one red shoe and one cement overshoe.

Graphics a-fish-ionados will appreciate the fact that Berkeley Systems hired a professional artist to redo Tom and Ed's fish.

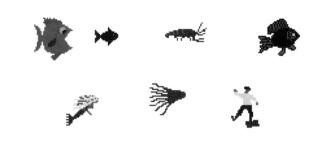

The two programmers, little realizing the fame and glory that the Fish! screen saver would one day bring them, placed their early Fish program on online bulletin boards, offering it free to anyone who cared to download it. They knew they were onto something when a number of people actually sent them checks for the program, even though it was offered as freeware rather than shareware (the latter is also distributed on computer bulletin boards, but programmers ask people who end up using their shareware programs to send them a small amount of money). Unfortunately, the two couldn't cash any of the checks, since Tom & Ed's Bogus Software wasn't an official company yet, but they considered the payments a nice tribute to their skills. Eventually, Tom & Ed's Bogus Software became a real company (although the two continue to hold day jobs), and Fish! evolved into a screen saver.

Sometime in 1989, Fish! caught the attention of the folks at Berkeley Systems, who contacted Tom and Ed about

including their screen saver in After Dark. Berkeley Systems hired artist Tomoya Ikeda to replace Tom and Ed's primitive fish with the beautiful renditions you see today. Fish! lets you choose among more than a dozen kinds of fish, and place as many as 50 fish on the screen at once.

Load Them Fishes   The Fish! module comes with an impressive set of fish, and More After Dark includes additional fish that you can import. If you want to create your own fish, you can order a Fish! Editor from Tom & Ed's Bogus Software for $19.95 (see the Fish! information screen for Tom & Ed's address). Although the Fish! Editor does indeed let you draw your own fish (or anything else you want swimming around in the Fish! module), be forewarned that you'll need quite a bit of patience to use the thing. You must draw your new fish dot-by-dot in the Fish! Editor's drawing window; unfortunately, you can't paste in graphics from a paint program.

Tom & Ed's Fish! Editor lets you create fish from scratch or import and edit existing After Dark fish.

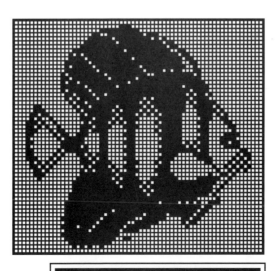

Sailfish Tang

21

Something Fishy Every now and then someone will call the Berkeley Systems technical support department to ask why there's a toaster winging its way through their on-screen aquarium. The answer is as follows: Fish! is located right above Flying Toasters in After Dark's alphabetical list of modules. Because the two modules are adjacent, every now and then an errant toaster makes its way into Fish! (Well, that's what they tell people, anyway. I'll leave it to the discerning reader to decide whether there's any truth to it.) Don't worry — the toaster won't electrocute the fish.

A note of caution to those of you who use screen savers during Mac-based classes. The president of a local software company related the following story to Berkeley Systems. The company was conducting a seminar to teach their salespeople about some of the firm's latest software. The instructor noticed that the people attending the class seemed awfully restless. Class members excused themselves from the room in record numbers, disrupting the seminar. Was it that boring? It was only in retrospect that the instructor realized that the Fish! screen saver had been running when the Macs were idle during the seminar; apparently the module's bubbling sound triggered a veritable exodus to the restrooms. Let that be a lesson to you: either turn down the sound or use another module if you teach a class.

Flying Toasters

There's something delightfully absurd about flying toasters. It's such a Salvador-Dalí-meets-Looney-Toons sort of idea, you just have to laugh. The winged appliance, which made its debut in After Dark 2.0, has pretty much become the program's mascot. Fans of this popular module might want to learn a little bit about how it came to be.

" It was a dark and stormy night. Well, chances are it wasn't stormy, since California was in the middle of a terrible drought at the time. But it was dark for sure. A lonely soul named Jack Eastman paced restlessly through his house. Actually, he wasn't all that lonely; he had a wife. But she was working the night shift, and he was indeed pacing around that night, trying to come up with an idea for a screen saver for the second version of After Dark. His pacing took him into the kitchen, and his eyes roamed across appliances large and small. Suddenly an idea popped into his head: "Flying toasters!" he exclaimed. He went upstairs, fired up Apple's resource editor ResEdit, and started making animated toaster icons. And the rest is history. Jack Eastman will forever be known, at least in some circles, as the Father of Flying Toasters. "

What caused such an image to come to mind? Before we elaborate on the development of the Flying Toasters module, we should point out that flying toasters are deeply rooted in the Greco-Roman tradition (although few scholars are willing to acknowledge their contribution to Western Civilization). As such, they are ingrained in the modern psyche and cannot be ignored as a cultural icon. The following section will place flying toasters in the proper socio-historical perspective. (If you're of a practical bent, you can skip to the end of this section for tips on using the Flying Toasters module.)

Flying Toasters and the Collective Unconscious To the Ancient Greeks, the flying toaster symbolized the melding of Art (the wings) and Science (the toaster), the twin cornerstones of their culture.

The Greek goddess of toast was Athena, who sprang, fully-formed, from the forehead of Zeus (the connection to toast is obvious). Athena was also known, peripherally, as the goddess of wisdom. The god of toast was Hermes (known as Mercury to the Romans). His trademark winged sandals and helmet symbolized the speedy egress of the toasted bread (the soul) from its warm and uncomfortable prison (the body). Figure 1 illustrates the influence of Hermes on modern-day toaster art, which reached its peak in the late 1800s, in the work of the European Toast-Impressionists. (Toast also pops up in paintings from the Dark Ages, the Middle Ages, and the Age of Enlightenment; unfortunately, most examples were burned by Savonarola and his band of reformists.)

Daedalus is generally considered to be the inventor of the flying toaster, although some researchers dispute this theory. The dubious reader is encouraged to consult Figure 2, a bas-relief from the frieze on the Temple at Tostopolis, which clearly shows Daedalus, seated on a cooler (another of his inventions), affixing a wing to a toaster. His son, Icarus, assists by steadying the wing. Although History does not tell us whether Daedalus' toasters actually flew, one can surmise that they probably fared no better than Icarus, whose wax-and-feather wings, you'll recall, melted when he flew too close to the sun.

Now that you understand the cultural significance of flying toasters, it's time to return to the present day.

FIGURE 1   *The tie between Greek mythology and flying toasters is obvious. The god Hermes is shown here; Dionysus was also a prominent influence, as he often raised his wineglass in a festive toast.*

FIGURE 2   *The Greek inventor Daedalus is thought by many to have constructed the first flying toaster.*

The Evolution of Flying Toasters Jack Eastman's original toasters were, to put it charitably, primitive. For starters, he was constrained by ResEdit to a grid only 32 pixels wide and 32 pixels high, and was limited to black and white. But despite these limitations — and his confessed lack of artistic talent — Jack persevered. The prototoasters' stubby wings looked a bit like those of a plucked chicken. Jack's original Flying Toaster module can be found on the disk that comes with this book.

See the "Art of Darkness Modules" section later in this chapter for details.

Jack kept enhancing his early version of Flying Toasters. The first improvement was the addition of toast. Compared to his toasters, Jack's toast wasn't too bad; after all, just about anyone can draw toast (or is that "draw a bath"? Household items confuse me sometimes).

Toaster Physics   To keep the program's size and memory requirements down, Jack decided that the flying objects shouldn't cross over one another. [Fish, unlike toasters, can overlap, as you know from viewing After Dark's Fish! module, but to explain the phenomena responsible for this behavioral difference is, alas, beyond the scope of this monograph; interested readers should consult the excellent article "Comparative Physiography of the Common Brook Trout and Raisin Toast," Hamilton et al., *Popular Appliance*, May 1973.] So he figured out a way to make the toasters weave around one other, rather than overlap.

When he had a working version of Toasters, Jack showed it to the folks at Berkeley Systems. They liked it. But the program was in the "runs good, needs work" stage, and Jack didn't have time to keep improving it, since he was working on the core program for After Dark 2.0. So he passed the project along to Patrick Beard, another programmer at Berkeley Systems. Patrick continued to refine the program, basically rewriting it. The two continued to share ideas as the program evolved, and — in a wonderful example of synergy — came up with my all-time favorite control: the toast darkness/lightness slider (available for color or gray-scale monitors). Neither can remember who thought it up, but when one of them tossed off the idea as a joke, the other seized on it and they decided they *had* to put it in. And they did, despite a looming deadline.

Other collaborative inventions include algorithmic toast darkening (much more efficient than drawing separate pieces of toast for each level of brownness) and the pioneering Toast Avoidance Algorithm, or TAA (pronounced *tah*), which ensures that toast and toasters don't collide.

The various programming enhancements would, of course, be of little value if the module shipped with Jack's stubby-winged graphics, so Berkeley Systems hired artist Tomoya Ikeda to draw the final toasters. And a fine job he did, too; fewer sights are more beautiful (in *my* office, anyway) than white wings reflected in the chrome sides of a flock of toasters!

As a final touch, the programmers added the sounds of flapping wings (imagine, if you will, a Berkeley Systems executive frantically flapping file folders, while other employees recorded the sounds); several samples were artfully combined and shuffled by Patrick to give the toasters their random flapping noise.

For tips on combining Flying Toasters with other modules, see Chapter 3. To learn how to modify toaster graphics, see Chapter 4.

Ann Crampton of Berkeley Systems' international marketing department is no stranger to Flying Toasters. Among her other duties, Ann is custodian of Berkeley Systems' trade show mascot, a real-life toaster equipped with shiny metal wings. Once, when she was traveling to a trade show in Germany, a customs agent asked her what was in the cardboard box she was bringing into the country. "A flying toaster," she replied as nonchalantly as possible. "Huh?" was the agent's predictable reply. "You know," she said, "A toaster, with wings." Needless to say, she was asked to open the box. Imagine the official's astonishment when he saw she was telling the truth.

Hard Rain

Raindrops keep fallin' on my screen.... Hard Rain, by Jack Eastman, is one of the many rain-related After Dark modules you'll run across. It's this infernal drought, I tell you. Californians will do anything for some rain, even simulate it if necessary.

This module's sliders let you set the number of drops that fall at once, as well as the maximum drop life (how big a drop can get).

Trivia: The "fr" in the Max Drop Life slider stands for frames, as in frames of an animation. The more frames a drop has, the larger it is. Now if that isn't trivial, I don't know what is.

Lissajous

This module lets you create different Lissajous patterns. What are Lissajous patterns?, inquiring readers might ask. Well, I called up the reference librarian to find out. She'd forgiven me by this time for my inane question about the Coriolis effect (see the section on Down the Drain), and she promptly and cheerfully informed me that they were named after the French mathematician Jules Antoine Lissajous, who studied wave motion in the 1800s. Programmer Patrick Beard told me that Lissajous patterns were a type of pattern you could create on an oscilloscope. I spent many happy hours as a child playing with my dad's oscilloscope in his workshop, but now I've put away nerdish things, and couldn't tell you much about oscilloscopes. However, I can share with you some of my favorite Lissajous slider settings (look at the Lissajous info screen for some of Patrick Beard's faves):

- 3, $\sqrt{3}$, 63, 100 ("Tail Chaser")

- 0, 1, 0, 0 ("TV Off")

- 2, 1, 29, 0 ("Saturn")

- 4, 2, 13, 7 ("Tinkerbell")

Logo

This module, written by Jack Eastman and Rob Vaterlaus, lets you use your own graphic as a screen saver. It doesn't have to be a logo, of course; you can use any picture created with a graphics application such as MacPaint, SuperPaint or Canvas. Or, if you're not the artistic type, use a scanned image (saved in paint or PICT format) or a picture from a Macintosh clip art collection.

If the image you want to use is in a graphics format other than PICT or paint, you can convert it to PICT format in a number of ways. For example, if you have an image in the TIFF file format (Tagged-Image File Format, a popular format for scanned images) or the EPS format (Encapsulated PostScript, a common format for Mac clip art), you can open the image with an application that supports EPS or TIFF. Such applications include paint/draw programs such as SuperPaint, PostScript graphics programs such as Aldus FreeHand or Adobe Illustrator, or page-layout applications like QuarkXPress or Aldus PageMaker. Once you've imported the picture into one of these programs, you can use the program's selection tool to copy the image to the Mac's Scrapbook, where it will be saved as a PICT file. You can then reopen the image — now in PICT format — with a graphics program that supports PICT (I use Aldus SuperPaint) and fine-tune it. You may want to add a black background, for example, or embellish the picture with the program's drawing tools. (Note: You can also open a screen-shot file with Apple's TeachText [version 7 or later], an application that's included with many programs so you can read on-disk additions to their manuals.) When you've finished tweaking your picture, use your program's selection tool to grab just the part you want, then select Copy from the Edit menu. This copies the selection to the Mac's Clipboard.

After you've copied your picture to the Clipboard, immediately open Logo and click the module's Pictures button.

The following dialog box will appear:

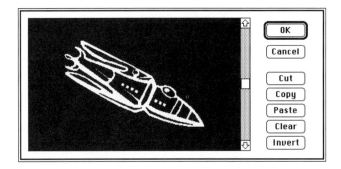

Click the Paste button, and the image you just copied to the Clipboard will appear in Logo's graphics window. (You can store a collection of images in Logo; just click the arrow in this window's scroll bar to move from one picture to another.) If necessary, click the Invert button to place the picture on a black background.

Caution: Make sure you mean it when you press the Clear button in this dialog box; doing so will obliterate the currently displayed image.

With the picture you want for your logo displayed in the window, click the OK button to return to Logo's main control panel. Now, when Logo is activated, the selected picture will float around the screen at the rate you've selected with the Float Speed slider.

Messages

Colin Glassey's Messages, which is based on an earlier version by Bruce Burkhalter, lets you display custom messages on your screen. You can type in anything you wish via the Edit Message button, and set attributes such as font, style, and size. A slider lets you set the speed at which the message will display, and a pop-up menu gives you three display styles: the message can pop up at various places on the screen, float around the screen, or scroll across horizontally as though it's coming off a teletypewriter. The latter option lets you include a teletype sound effect if you wish.

Messages can provide a practical way to let people know where you are ("In a meeting; back at 3:30") or provide an invaluable means of creative expression ("I think that I shall never see/A fully clad female on MTV").

MultiModule
This module, which lets you combine After Dark modules into custom creations, is discussed in detail in the next chapter.

NightLines
This module, by Jim Bailey, draws symmetrical or asymmetrical lines on the screen. That's about all I have to say about that. If you think you can come up with something clever or informative to say about a module that draws a bunch of lines on the screen, then write your own After Dark book, dang it!

PICS Player
The PICS Player module, by Rob Vaterlaus and Bruce Burkhalter, lets you view screen-saving cartoons that float across your monitor. Said 'toons must be in PICS format, a common format for Mac animations. If you have an animation program such as MacroMind Director, AddMotion, Animation Works, or Cinemation, you can create your own PICS-format animations for this module. If you don't have an animation program, you can purchase a collection of PICS animations such as Media In Motion's Animation Clips. Several companies offer CD ROMs full of multimedia clips, including PICS files. If you don't have an animation program or the money to buy commercial PICS clips (statistics show that low-income, non-animation-program-owning adults make up a large percentage of the population), then you might want to log on to an online

bulletin board and download some free PICS animations, or contact your local Macintosh user group (BMUG, the Berkeley Mac user group, offers a collection of PICS animations for $15). If you don't have access to any of the aforementioned resources, then I'm afraid you're just going to have to use some other module.

Since many animations exist on a white background, while After Dark favors a black one, the module offers an Invert option that changes white to black and vice versa in an animation. This looks better than an animation that's floating around in a white rectangle, but switching black lines to white ones can make a drawing look a little odd. For better results, change a sequence's background to black in an animation program.

Unfortunately, since the PICS format doesn't support sound, your PICS Player displays will lack soundtracks. But your silent-movie days are over if you have Apple's Quick-Time. The Movies 'Til Dawn module that comes with this book allows you to play QuickTime movies — including PICS animations — sound and all. (Movies 'Til Dawn is described later in this chapter.)

Picture Frame

This module, by Patrick Beard and Colin Glassey, lets you use a color PICT file as your screen saver (see the earlier section on the Logo module for an explanation of PICT files). Simply put any PICT files you want to use in the Slide Show Folder in your After Dark Files folder. Then select the file you want with Picture Frame's Choose Picture button.

Since using a static image as a screen saver is counterproductive, Picture Frame offers an Intensity slider that lets you dim the picture on a color monitor.

Puzzle

The Puzzle module, by Bruce Burkhalter and John Rotenstein, divides whatever's on your screen into a series of squares (small, medium, or large) and proceeds to rearrange them in the manner of those old-fashioned puzzles made up of sliding plastic tiles. You can use this module as a pleasant diversion, or perhaps to turn the contents of a word-processor document into surrealist poetry. In addition to tile size, this module lets you set the puzzle's speed, invert the screen, and apply a satisfying "click" sound when the tiles move.

This module is decorative, rather than interactive. If you want to actually solve a puzzle, try Apple's Puzzle desk accessory, or maybe After Dark's Snake module (described later in this chapter).

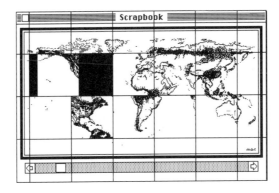

Rainstorm

Yet another soggy module, this one by Patrick Beard. You can assume the role of a divine power and set the intensity of the storm, the delay between lightning flashes, and how far away the storm is. With a little prodding, I finally remembered the formula I'd used in my long-lost youth to calculate the distance of a thunderstorm: when you see a flash of lightning, count slowly, "one thousand one…one thousand two," and so on for each second; every count of five seconds equals one mile. Stop counting when you hear the thunder. Sure enough, this module lives up to Berkeley Systems' high standards of scientific accuracy. Set the Storm Distance slider to 1 mile, for example, and start counting when the lightning flashes on your screen. After five seconds, a peal of thunder will sound.

Randomizer

Like MultiModule (which is described in the next chapter), Patrick Beard's Randomizer operates in conjunction with other After Dark modules. Randomizer lets you select a set of modules and display them in random order, or alphabetical order if you prefer. (See Chapter 4 for a tip on rearranging the order of the modules in After Dark's scrolling list.)

To set up a Randomizer sequence, open the module and click the Choose button. The first time you open it, you'll see that a number of modules are already highlighted in Randomizer's scrolling list. You can deselect a module by clicking its name, or deselect the entire bunch by holding down the mouse button and running the cursor down the list. Click on the names of the modules you want to include in your Randomizer sequence.

In the Randomizer control panel, set the Order option to Random or In Order (the latter displays the selected modules in alphabetical order), and set the Duration slider to the amount of time you want each module to display.

Note: Randomizer employs a universal sound control. No matter what volume you've set within each module, Randomizer will play sounds at the volume level set in the Randomizer control panel. (If you've turned off the sound in an individual module, however, Randomizer won't play it.)

Hey Kids! If you have kids, they can use Randomizer to create a swell spaceship simulation. A Berkeley Systems employee told me of two youngsters who, with the help of a little cardboard and tape, set up a Mac to be the bridge of a starship. They used Randomizer to view combinations of Warp!, Globe, Mountains, Supernova, and other spacey modules.

Rose

Like a giddy swarm of fireflies wafted on a warm summer zephyr, the dots in this lovely module sweep and swirl across your screen. (Warning: Staring at this module for too long may cause you to write in a wistful and sentimental style. I suspect that's because it's so beautiful.)

Sliders let you set the display speed and trail length, while check boxes let you specify large or small dots and whether to run the module in color. (Try big dots, no trails.)

Satori

Ben Haller's Satori creates a shimmering swirl of color on your screen. It creates a shimmering swirl of grays if you have a gray-scale monitor. Alas, Satori doesn't work at all on black-and-white screens. That's because it uses a technique called *color cycling* to shift the colors in the display; since there are no shades or colors on a black-and-white Mac, color cycling won't work.

Satori offers quite a few controls. The Display pop-up menu gives you a choice of basic shapes, such as Waves or Leaves. The Colors menu offers a range of palettes, from the warm, desert hues of Arizona to the cool blues of Siberia. Press the Caps Lock key to change colors while Satori is running.

The End Resolution slider determines how fine the display will be; the smaller the number, the more detailed the display. The Knots slider increases or decreases the complexity of the display.

Tip: Place this module behind others in MultiModule to create some wild and wonderful color effects.

Shapes

See the above entry for NightLines, and substitute the word "shapes" for "lines." (And the word "Jack" for "Jim," and "Eastman" for "Bailey.")

Slide Show

Colin Glassey's Slide Show lets you display a series of images. A slider allows you to set the length of time each image will be displayed, anywhere from 5 seconds to an hour. (Most slide shows are boring enough without making the audience watch each slide for an hour, but one assumes that this setting is for people who simply want to change their screen display several times a day.)

The Intensity slider lets owners of color or gray-scale monitors set the brightness of the images, while the Fade Speed slider controls how fast one image fades out and the next comes up to its full intensity.

To set up a slide show, first create a collection of images in the PICT format. (If you're not familiar with the PICT format, refer to the earlier description of the Logo module.) Place your pictures in the Slide Show folder, which is located in the After Dark Files folder. The pictures are displayed in alphabetical order; you can put the slides in any order you wish simply by clicking on the PICT files in the Slide Show folder and re-naming them. If you prefer, you can place a number before each slide's name to set the sequence in which they're shown.

Spheres

The Spheres module, by the indefatigable Bruce Burkhalter, draws three-dimensional-looking spheres on the screen. Set the Offset amount to 10 and you'll get egglike shapes instead of spheres.

Combine Spheres (with the aforementioned ovoid Offset of 10 and a maximum size of 10%) with Confetti Factory in a MultiModule to create a Confetti-and-Easter-Egg Factory. (This one's especially precious when the Confetti-Factory ducks walk by.)

Spotlight

Turn your Mac's desktop into a gala Hollywood opening with Spotlight, written by Bruce Burkhalter and Rob Vaterlaus, from an idea by Bob Schumaker and Chip Morningstar.

This module lets you set the number of spotlights, their size, and how quickly they play across the screen.

Starry Night

Starry Night is After Dark's default module, the one that kicks in if a selected module fails to run for some reason (a memory problem or a monitor set to the wrong number of colors for a given module, for example). It displays a city skyline against a night sky.

Starry Night is built into the program (hence its unalphabetical appearance at the top of the program's list of modules). It doesn't have a corresponding file in the After Dark Files folder, so you can't remove it, change its order in the menu, or make a copy. Similarly, Starry Night can't be used as part of a MultiModule. If you have a hankering to use a night skyline in a MultiModule, you can use Starry Night's close relative, Starry Skyline, which is described in the next entry.

Starry Skyline

Starry Skyline, by Jack Eastman, is similar to After Dark's default module, Starry Night, but offers the functionality you'd expect from an After Dark module. You can set the number of buildings in the skyline, as well as the buildings' maximum height. A checkbox lets you display a flasher if you wish (no, it's not a demented city dweller in an overcoat, but rather a flashing light on top of one of the taller buildings to warn passing aircraft).

The only airborne objects you're likely to see in Starry Skyline (unless you get creative with a MultiModule) are shooting stars (or incoming missiles, if you have that sort of imagination), which zoom by with a whooshing sound.

String Theory

Very much like the String Art module (see the "More After Dark Modules" section), but more theoretical.

Supernova

This module, by the prolific Jack Eastman, depicts a cosmic explosion. Unlike most After Dark modules, this one has no controls. But, after all, what sort of control could one have over an exploding star?

In keeping with this module's cosmic theme, I combined it in a MultiModule with Major Metaphysical Appliances, one of the new modules included with this book. The results were most spectacular.

Vertigo

Like the Satori module, which was described earlier, Jack Eastman's Vertigo uses color cycling to produce an ever-changing array of colors. And, like Satori, Vertigo won't work with a black-and-white screen.

Vertigo lets you set the shapes that will be displayed:

spirals, circles, squares, or zooms (the latter look like three-dimensional cones), or a combination of shapes if Random is chosen. Sliders control the tightness of the spirals and the length of time each Vertigo display lasts.

For a good time, combine with other modules in Multi-Module.

Warp!

This module, written by Bruce Burkhalter, puts armchair space cadets at the helm of a rocket that's hurtling through the void (or moseying through the void if you set the Speed slider to 1 or 2). In addition to your warp speed, you can set the size, number, and color of the module's stars.

Zot!

This module, by Jack Eastman and Colin Glassey, puts an electrical storm on your screen. Sliders control the lightning's Kinkiness (how straight or jagged the main bolt will be), Forkiness (how many forks will appear), and Delay between strikes. If you have a color monitor, you can check a box for colored lightning, but I find that this adversely affects the module's realism.

More After Dark Modules

This section describes the 26 modules that make up More After Dark, a series of add-on modules for After Dark.

Boris

A lot of work went into Boris the cat, one of More After Dark's most popular modules. Rob Vaterlaus did the programming portion of Boris, while Igor Gasowski did the artwork. Boris includes 200 individual frames, 100 each for the color version and the black-and-white version.

A good deal of debate went into just what sort of cat Boris should be. Some people lobbied for a cartoonish cat, while others wanted a more realistic one. The current Boris is somewhat of a compromise between these two styles; he's a cute little guy, but exhibits some very convincing catlike behavior (scratching the side of the monitor, for example).

Here are just a few of the multitude of sketches and prototypes that went into Boris' development:

Boris works very well in MultiModules with most After Dark and More After Dark modules. That's partly because he's programmed to pass in front of other objects without obscuring them. Chapter 3 presents several ideas for using Boris in MultiModules; Chapter 4 describes how to modify Boris' sound effects.

Confetti Factory

Ever wonder how confetti was made? I thought not. Confetti Factory, by Paul Young and Mouse Herrell, with artwork by Igor Gasowski, juxtaposes an element of frivolity (confetti) with the harsh reality of post-industrial society (conveyor belts and gears). The resulting mixture of gloom and levity has been known to bring tears to the eyes of aesthetically sensitive viewers.

After a Confetti Factory workshift is over (you can set the Workshift slider to as high as 10 minutes if you're a hard taskmaster), a cadre of ducks marches onto the screen (unless, of course, you've set the Number of Ducks slider to 0). As the Marx Brothers asked so long ago, "Why a duck?" The answer is simple in this case. If the conveyor belts stayed on the screen for hours, they might contribute to screen burn-in rather than help prevent it. After the ducks go by (or don't go by, if they're on strike), the factory returns in a new configuration.

Tip: Press the Caps Lock key to reverse the direction of the conveyor belts.

Question: Let's say you were a somewhat conservative reveler, and only threw one tiny scrap of paper. (I can think of somebody mentioned in this book who might fit that description.) Would it be a *confetto*? I really don't have the nerve to call that poor reference librarian again; it's questions like this that cause otherwise even-tempered people to snap. Perhaps a reader could find out and let me know for a future edition.

Dominoes

If you're short on leisure time (and these days, who isn't?), you can let the Mac do your relaxing for you with Patrick Beard's Dominoes. This module plays a game of dominoes with wooden or ivory pieces. (Don't worry; since this is a computer simulation, only simulated ivory was used.)

GeoBounce

Can you say "dodecahedron"? Even if you can't, you can bounce one around your screen with Ed Hall's GeoBounce. This module lets you select the shape (4, 6, 8, 12, or 20 faces), size, and speed of a 3-D object that caroms off the sides of the screen with a very satisfying *thwock* sound. You can set your shape to any hue you choose by pressing the Set Color button.

Trivia: In Demo mode, the GeoBounce shape bounces off the module's control-panel window as well as the edges of the screen.

Globe

Globe, by Jack Eastman, can be the star of your screen saver collection if you put a little work into it. This module originally comes up as a spinning Earth, but you can apply a picture of anything to the surface of the sphere.

To use your own graphic, first open a picture in TeachText or a graphics program. Select the image and choose Copy from the Edit menu to place it in the Clipboard. Next, open Globe and click the Image button. The following dialog box will appear:

Click the Paste button, and the image you just copied will appear in the image window. Click OK to return to Globe's control panel, then click the Demo button. Your custom graphic will automatically wrap itself around the globe. (If you don't have a graphic handy, you can see a quick demonstration of Globe's capabilities by dragging the slider to the top of the image window, where you'll see the words "Use whatever is on your screen." Click OK and Globe will cover itself with whatever's displayed at the time.)

Sliders let you set the globe's rotation speed and the position of its shadow. Check the Orbiting box if you want the globe to move around the screen.

Tip: Although Globe will automatically resize an image if necessary, for best results you should copy an image that's about the size of the map in Globe's image window.

GraphStat

This goofy module by Harry Chesley pretends to display various graphs on your Mac's screen. As the module's info box states, "GraphStat will...produce beautiful graphs with absolutely no data entry. Think of the time you'll save."

GraphStat allows you to customize the graph labels, making them, for instance, pertain to your company's business. With a little work, you can also edit the labels so GraphStat displays statistics that refer specifically to your friends or coworkers. Examples include "Jay's Attention Span [minutes]" or "Edna's Level of Obnoxiousness [exponential]." You can also use GraphStat to write random poetry. Simply replace the existing phrases with words of your own.

First, go into the After Dark Files folder and make a copy of GraphStat (see page 78 for instructions on copying modules). Because GraphStat randomly combines a first, second, and third phrase, as well as an optional subtitle for each graph, you'll have to clear the decks by clicking Edit Labels and then deleting the existing labels in your copy of the module. You can do this fairly quickly by clicking the Delete button repeatedly, as fast as you can hit the mouse button. When you've deleted all the first-phrase entries, click the New button and type the word (or words) of your choice for the first phrase. Do the same for the subsequent phrases, and the subtitle if you wish. Now, when GraphStat comes up, it will display your custom label.

Gravity

You've heard the expression "That's the way the ball bounces." But until now, you probably haven't had the means at your disposal to illustrate this saying with a computer simulation. Thanks to More After Dark, you can put as many as 50 bouncing balls on your screen.

Sliders let you set the number of balls that will appear, as well as their size (from Weensy to Huge). Balls leave trails behind them if you check the Trails box, and boing off one another if you check Collisions.

In Gravity, the bigger they are, the slower they fall. Also, selecting a large number of balls slows down the action. If you select 50 huge balls, they bounce fairly slowly. For a spritely display, exercise a little moderation in the size and number of balls.

Life II

Life II is programmer Ben Haller's rendition of a popular program developed by John Conway in the late 1960s. Conway's Life was an attempt to show that complex behavior could emerge from a simple set of rules. Basically, Life consists of a group of cells that exist in an invisible grid. The behavior of each cell is determined by the eight cells that surround it. During each time step of the game, the configuration of the cells on the grid will change, depending on the interaction between each cell and its neighbors. Life is an example of what's called a *cellular automaton*, since its cells exhibit behavior that makes them seem almost like a living organism.

Cells can be either alive or dead; if a cell is alive, it will survive a given time step if either two or three adjacent cells are alive. Cells are finicky about the conditions they need to stay alive; if more than three of a cell's neighbors are alive, it will die of overcrowding, while if only one neighbor is alive — or no neighbors at all — it will die of loneliness.

If a cell has died, it will stay dead unless three of its neighbors are alive, in which case it will revive.

Because the conditions during each time step affect those of the following step, Life can become a seething soup of activity as cells are born and die, affecting an intricate web of interactions between neighboring cells.

As you'll see if you run Life II for a bit, sometimes groups of cells will stabilize into certain patterns. Conway and his colleagues gave the common patterns names, based on objects they resembled, such as longboat, beehive, or block. Patterns can be stable, or they can oscillate between two states. For example, a block of four cells — two on the top row and two on the bottom — will simply sit there forever unless another cell or group of cells happens to run into it and start things moving again. Three cells stacked vertically — like a traffic light — will continually oscillate between that position and a horizontal configuration.

Other patterns do more interesting things. Perhaps the most famous of Life's creations are the gliders. These critters shift their shape for several steps, moving across the screen as they deviate from their original shape and then return to it.

In After Dark, you can do more than just watch Life pass you by. By pressing the Caps Lock key, you can enter the game's interactive mode and tinker with the game's cell structures. When you're in interactive mode, you can draw with the cursor. Click on a blank part of the screen to draw a cell, or click on an existing cell to erase it. To start with a blank slate, press the N key to get a new file. You can try drawing a simple pattern to see what it turns into, or write your name in cells and see what sort of egocentric lifeform evolves. Press the Tab key to move one generation at a time. If you like what you see, you can press the S key to save your Life file; you can't use the Mac's normal file-naming methods, but instead must press a number key from 1 to 9 to name the file. You can then open that file by pressing the O key, or paste it into another Life file by pressing the P key. Press Caps Lock again to go from interactive mode to Life II (although you can use the mouse and keyboard in interactive mode, touching either of these while Life II is running will quit the game).

Life was one of the first examples of a new field called *artificial life,* in which latter-day mad scientists are trying to understand some of the properties of real life by creating simulated creatures or ecosystems on their computers. After attending the third Artificial Life Conference, I'm sorry to report that nobody's come up with a compterized creature yet that could actually be called *alive,* but they're making some progress. Many of the current crop of simulated critters can develop methods for finding food (lo-cal stuff made up of binary digits, or *bits*), "mate" with other simulated critters (the naughty bits), or even evolve strategies for coping with their worlds, exhibiting behaviors that weren't specifically programmed into them. If you're interested in learning about A-life, I'd highly recommend Steven Levy's book *Artificial Life: The Quest for a New Creation* (Pantheon, 1992).

Note: Life II works in black and white, but looks best with 256 colors.

Lunatic Fringe

Twenty years of schoolin', and I'm writing tips about spaceship shoot-'em-ups. Oh well. Beats working.

I've spent more time than I care to admit playing Lunatic Fringe, the highly addictive game that's included with More After Dark. At first I felt guilty for frittering away so many precious hours killing space aliens, when I could have been reading Proust, learning to play the mandolin, or otherwise bettering myself. Then, slowly but steadily, the rationalizations began to kick in. After all, Lunatic Fringe is not merely a game, but a way to actively involve the computer user in the screen-saving process. Besides, shooting aliens develops hand-eye coordination and hones one's motor skills. When I began working on this book, I came to my crowning rationalization: "I'm getting paid for this." But you can't use that one, gentle reader. Think up your own.

If you spend an inordinate amount of time playing Lunatic Fringe, you've probably figured out many of the following tips. If not, read on. This section is guaranteed to increase your score by at least nine skill levels.

- Are you embarrassed when your Lunatic Fringe score display reveals that you've only made it to level 4 or 5? Well, you can remedy that situation right away by double-clicking the After Dark icon, selecting the Lunatic Fringe module, and setting the Starting Level slider to level 10. This not only makes you look less wimpy to passers-by, but gives you immediate access to all the nasty characters in the Fringe; no more waiting around for the Slicer to make its terrifying debut.

- Be very careful, when you're in the midst of a Lunatic Fringe game, not to touch the mouse. As you've probably learned from bitter experience, doing so will immediately kill the game and return you to reality.

- The closer you get to an alien ship, the better your chances of blowing it to smithereens. If you dare, position yourself nose-to-nose with the enemy ship before firing.

- You may have used your turbo-thrust to flee a sticky situation. But the turbo-thrust isn't just for flight; it can also be used to fight. The next time you're losing a shootout, aim your ship *at* the enemy instead of away from it, and punch the turbo-thrust button. You'll have yet another dead alien on your conscience.

- You know the feeling: you've lost your turn jets and you're spinning aimlessly through the void, unable to pick a direction or maintain a steady course. Lord knows, I often feel that way even when I'm not playing Lunatic Fringe…but I digress. You can still move around when your ship's turn jets are damaged. Just hit the gas every time the ship points in the direction you want to go, and you'll limp along through space—albeit in a loopy sort of way. If your turn jets are kaput and you need to shoot an attacking alien, wait until you're pointing in the right direction, then hold down the left and right turn buttons; this will stabilize your ship while you attempt to shoot your foe.

So, think you're good at Lunatic Fringe? The highest score I've ever heard of is Level 104, but I'll bet somebody out there has topped even that.

• The Slicer is not quite invincible. In addition to turning on your shield (assuming you haven't used it up) or using the aforementioned defensive thruster, you have a few options for killing this guy. The most elegant method is to head for an asteroid like a bat out of hell, then swerve at the last second, causing the pursuing Slicer to dash himself against the rock. An easier way is to pick a course, get your ship going at a good clip, then turn it around (without slowing down) to face the Slicer. As you're zipping backwards through space, you can shoot the Slicer at your leisure. This is so easy (unless you splatter yourself on a passing asteroid) that you almost feel sorry for the poor Slicer.

• Sorry, but there's no way to destroy the enemy base. So don't waste your ammo trying.

• Remember, you can pause the game by pressing the Caps Lock key. This is a good way to handle those pesky interruptions like phone calls or a roving boss.

This module was written by Ben Haller, refined under the watchful eye of Nick Rush, and illustrated by Igor Gasowski. Unlike other After Dark modules, it doesn't run in Demo mode or under MultiModule. (You can, however, include

Lunatic Fringe graphic elements in MultiModules. See Chapter 4 for details.)

Note: Lunatic Fringe requires a 1-bit (black-and-white) or 8-bit (256 colors) monitor setting to run.

Mandelbrot

Benoit Mandelbrot is considered to be the father of fractal geometry. (Who the mother is, I have no idea.) His book, *The Fractal Geometry of Nature* (aha, maybe she's the mother!) is a classic in the literature of mathematics and computer graphics. The word *fractal,* which was coined by Mandelbrot, comes from the Latin *fractus,* meaning fragmented or irregular. In a nutshell, fractals are shapes or patterns made up of ever-smaller versions of themselves (a characteristic often called self-similarity). It's easier to describe a fractal in pictures than in words, so take a look at Figure 3.

As you can see from the illustration, fractals can resemble shapes found in nature (the example shown here might remind you of a tree or a fern, for instance). Computer artists

FIGURE 3   *Fractals are made up of repetitions of the same elements. In this simple example, the basic shape is added to each line of the original drawing.*

49

have used fractals to create often-realistic renditions of natural objects such as snowflakes, clouds, mountains, and coastlines. (In fact, several other After Dark modules described in this book — Mountains, Fractal Forest, and Pearls — create images using fractal geometry.)

More After Dark's Mandelbrot module was created by Michael Hoffman and Jon Hartshorne. Although the module takes a while to draw the entire picture, you can learn a bit about how fractals work by watching how the program fills in the screen. Note how it creates smaller and smaller rectangles, filling each in as the graphic takes shape.

If you're running Mandelbrot in 256 colors, pressing the Caps Lock key changes the picture's color scheme.

Trivia: The "clut" mentioned in this module's info box stands for color lookup table, *a system used by computers for identifying and displaying colors.*

Plate 1 shows an example of More After Dark's Mandelbrot.

Meadow

Meadow is a relaxing module by Jack Eastman, with artwork by Igor Gasowski. Leave your Mac alone for a while, and your screen will blossom into a field of flowers.

You can set the starting season, as well as specify how long the seasons last. If you want an endless summer (or any other season, for that matter), set the Seasons Last slider to Forever.

See the following chapter for some ideas on how to use Meadow with MultiModule.

Modern Art

Seen on the wall of an art-school bathroom: "I know a lot about art, but I don't know what I like."

In this module by Jack Eastman and Bruce Burkhalter, the folks at Berkeley Systems deviate from their usual science and nature themes to give us an ever-so-brief lesson in art history. If you read Modern Art's info box, you'll learn that the three options pay homage to the Dutch painter Piet Mondrian and Americans Mark Rothko and Jackson "Jack the Dripper" Pollock.

You can pretend that your office is a trendy little coffeehouse by hanging copies of three Modern Artist modules — each set to a different artist and placed in a different screen location — in a MultiModule and displaying them on your monitor. (To add to the effect, you might want to wear a beret, leave a few novels by Émile Zola scattered around your desk, and boil the coffee in the office kitchenette for an extra hour or so and pretend it's capuccino.) Better yet, you can use After Dark to create your own artwork with MultiModule (see the next chapter for details).

Mountains

Mountains, by Ben Haller and Eli Meir, lets you simulate landscapes on the planet of your choice (or set the Planet control to Random and let the program pick the planets). This module offers a wide range of options, as it were. Use the module's menus to specify whether or not your planet has water and set the drawing style for the mountains (styles run from Frame, which produces just a scaffolding, to Solid, which fills every mountain facet with a solid shade). Sliders let you set Refinement (the higher the level, the more faces the mountains will have) and Zoom (a level of 100 gives you an aircraft's-eye view, while a level of 0 virtually places you in the landscape).

My favorite setting is the planet Saturn with water, the Sheet drawing style, a Refinement level of 5, and a Zoom setting of 40. On a color monitor, this combination gives you rosy, translucent mountains that resemble an ice palace at first light. (Actually, I've never seen an ice palace at first light, but I can dream, can't I?)

See the following chapter for a suggestion on using Mountains in a MultiModule.

51

Mowin' Man

This industrious module is the work of Glenn Corwin, who submitted it for the first After Dark module contest. In Mowin' Man, grass grows on your screen until a little fellow riding a mower rides in to trim it. This module is autobiographical; when Berkeley Systems called Glenn to tell him he was a contest winner, his wife had to call him in from mowing the lawn.

What I like about this module is the fact that, unlike my neighbor's Saturday morning mowing fests, one can turn down the sound of the Mowin' Man's power mower.

Nocturnes

This module, by Jon Steinmetz, has a terse info section: "Nocturnes scares children." To my credit, I didn't test this out (despite my generally rigorous research for this book), although my sentiments toward children are similar to those of Nancy Mitford, who said, "I love children, especially when they cry, for then someone takes them away."

Trivia: In the real world (as opposed to the screen saver world), you can tell what the temperature is by timing cricket chirps. Count the number of chirps you hear in 15 seconds, then add 40. The result is the temperature in degrees Farenheit.

Nocturnes presents a host of eerie nocturnal eyes, accompanied, if you turn on the sound, by chirping crickets and the occasional lonesome wolf wail. The module's Eyes slider goes from Sparse to Lots, but if even Lots of eyes aren't enough for you (perhaps you're attempting to scare a rather jaded child), you can always add more eyes by combining three or four Nocturnes modules into a MultiModule. (If you're unfamiliar with MultiModules, consult the next chapter.)

Corollary Trivia:
You can tell what
time it is by listen-
ing to a wolf's howl.
Time to go indoors!

(An After Dark user contacted Berkeley Systems to tell them of a strange problem. A raccoon had been trying to get into his house for several nights, and he couldn't figure out what was causing the beast's odd behavior. He finally realized that the raccoon was attracted to the sound of the crickets in his Nocturnes module, and was trying to get to them.)

Punchout

Punchout, by Rob Vaterlaus, applies the digital equivalent of cookie cutters to the contents of your screen. You can set the shape, size, and number of punchouts.

Combine Punchout with Puzzle in a MultiModule to really make a mess of your screen.

Rain

This module by Anthony Carlisle fills your screen with raindrops. You can set the Rain Amount from Drip to Downpour, and select the colors of your rain (multicolored, white, or a patriotic red, white, and blue). Even when the Rain Amount is set to Downpour, this module's much milder than its relatives Zot! and Rainstorm.

Ripple

Wes Boyd's Ripple simulates a moving pool of water, with real dynamic equations for wave motion. Monsieur Lissajous would have been proud! Sliders let you set the pool size and how often the drops fall. If you have a color monitor, you can use the Water Color button to select the color of your pool. If you wish, you can also opt to hear the drops plop.

I find this module very soothing, but it could conceivably be used as a sort of modern-day Chinese water torture for people with desks near yours.

53

Say What?

This module by Jim Miars gives you the chance to make your Mac a bulletin board of wit and wisdom.

The module comes with an eclectic collection of 198 humorous quotes from sages such as Mark Twain, W. Somerset Maugham, and Snoopy. You can specify how long each quote will be displayed (from 10 to 100 seconds), as well as whether it will appear in a border.

If you tire of the module's selection of quotes, you can add your own pearls of wisdom: your personal observations, memorable lines from fellow workers, additional quotes from famous people, or perhaps a line of Shakespeare or Donne to brighten your dreary workday. Just press the Edit Quotes button in the Say What? control panel, then click the New button in the window that appears. You can type as many new quotes as you like, as well as delete existing ones you don't like. If you wish, you can change the font and font size in which the module's quotes will appear.

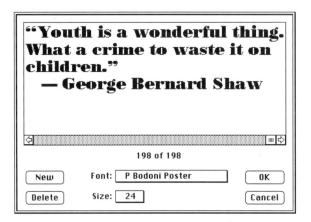

Snake

Which is faster, a Macintosh computer or the human brain? Snake, by Jim Miars, gives you the chance to find out, as you try to beat a computerized snake as it wends its way through a maze.

PLATE 1

Mandelbrot (see page 49)

PLATE 2

Fractal Forest (see page 60)

PLATE 3

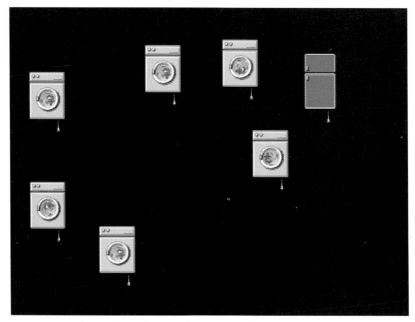

Major Metaphysical Appliances (see page 60)

PLATE 4

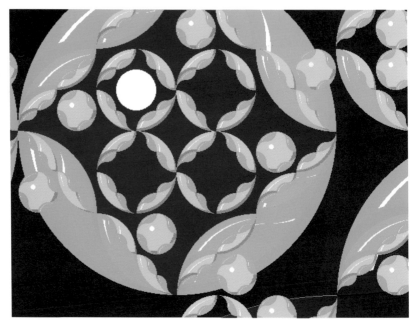

Pearls (see page 62)

PLATE 5

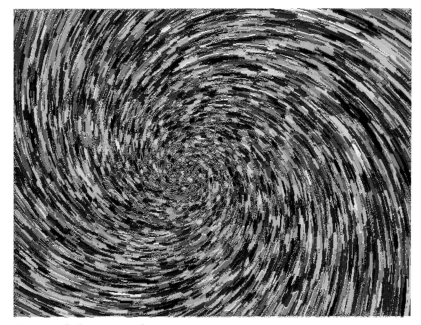

Spin Brush (see page 64)

PLATE 6

Strange Attractors (see page 65)

PLATE 7

SunBurst (see page 66)

PLATE 8

Clockwork Vertigo (see page 84)

Computers may be fast, but us humans still call the shots, at least as far as this module is concerned. If you set the Solution Speed slider (which determines how fast the computer solves the maze) to a low number, and the Maze Complexity slider to a low number as well, chances are you can beat the thing. This module provides a stimulating way to clear your monitor of dust (and replace it with grease from your finger) as you frantically trace possible routes on the screen.

Of course, if you're feeling lazy, you can simply watch the Snake figure out the maze.

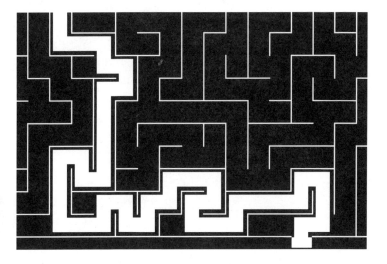

Spiral Gyra

I can't think of much to say about Spiral Gyra, a perfectly nice module by Keith Alphonso and John Casey (I have trouble with these liney ones). It's a mesmerizing module that draws swooping loops and twisting lines. I *can* tell you, however, that the word *mesmerize* comes from the Austrian physician Franz Anton Mesmer (1734–1815), who was able to hypnotize his patients without even using a screen saver.

For a dazzling MultiModule, combine Spiral Gyra with Stained Glass.

Stained Glass

Stained Glass, by Jean Tantra, creates scintillating patterns of colored lines and shapes (or black-and-white lines and shapes if you have a monochrome monitor). The module offers sliders for the following characteristics: Complexity (from 0 to 100), Duplication (from 0 to 100) and Color (also from 0 to 100). If you read the module's info box (press the triangle in the lower-right corner of the module's control panel), you'll see the following phrase: "We don't understand the controls either." Thanks a lot, Berkeley Systems.

Well, I don't understand them either, so I called Mr. Tantra, who shed a little light on Stained Glass. Unfortunately, even he didn't understand the controls, since the programmers at Berkeley Systems fiddled with the program he submitted to them. But he did tell me that he has an interest in quilting, and that that's where some of the ideas for Stained Glass came from. The module draws a "patch" in the center of the screen, then creates a number of tiles based on that patch, which makes many of the screens look a lot like patchwork quilts.

He also gave me some information on the more than 200 variables that make up the module's drawing rules (shapes used, direction of drawing, tiling routines, number of tiles, odd or even pixel patterns, border color, and so on), but to describe these would be beyond the scope of this book [that's technical-writer talk for "I don't understand any of this in the least"].

As near as Jean and I could figure, the Color slider sets the number of colors, from black-and-white at the left to. . .er, lots of colors at the right. The Complexity slider determines, well, complexity. As for the Duplication slider, your guess is as good as ours.

Now before you go running out to get a refund on this book, just finish this paragraph. I agree that I'm not of much help on this particular module. But I can offer a bit of advice that applies not only to After Dark, but to the Vast Cosmic Scheme of Things as well: If you don't understand how

Trivia: Stained Glass uses a random number generator to seed its patterns. The programmer estimates that you might see a repeated display in a billion years or so.

something works, experiment and see what you can find out. (Come to think of it, you might not want to apply this piece of advice to, say, figuring out what makes your pet hamster tick, but you get the idea.) Alas, a lot of us grownups have forgotten how to play — except for the occasional game of office politics, but who needs that? After Dark offers a great opportunity to play, and if some curmudgeonly supervisor gets on your case, explain that you're saving the company money by optimizing a series of modules that prevent potential damage to expensive raster-based monitors.

Stained Glass has grown to be one of my favorite modules; I find it very relaxing to watch the nearly endless variety of patterns. (The module's original name was Art Therapy, since the programmer found it so soothing to watch.)

For tips on using Stained Glass in MultiModules, see the next chapter.

String Art

Very much like String Theory (see the "After Dark Modules" section), but more arty.

Terraform

Brian Lowry's Terraform gives you an aerial view of a variety of landscapes. The module's info box states that "if you look closely you can read the license plate off a KGB vehicle." I haven't seen one yet, but I'm pretty sure I spotted Elvis sitting in a lawn chair on a small island.

The Repeat Size menu determines how large to make the squares, or tiles, that make up each image. The larger the repeat size, the less repetition a landscape will display. The Idle Time slider sets the number of seconds between displays.

Click the Terrain button to customize your Terraform views. You can customize not only the land, but water and cloud configurations as well. The module lets you choose specific settings or optionally display settings at random.

If you have a color monitor, you'll find that the Neon terrain setting creates landscapes with an uncanny resemblance to infrared satellite photos.

See Chapter 4 for a unique way to modify Terraform.

Tunnel

There is a light at the end of the Tunnel, but only if you run this module in 256 colors or grays. Tunnel, by Darin Gurney and Mouse Herrell, takes you on a dizzying ride through tunnels of various shapes: oval, rectangle, or rounded-corner rectangle. If you start to feel claustrophobic, you can always change the direction from In to Out.

Note: Although a picture will display on a black-and-white monitor, it will be stationary.

Virex-D

This virus detector, which was bundled with the first release of More After Dark, is not only useful, but fun to watch. It draws 3-D versions of icons that reside on your Mac, then passes a beam of light over each icon as it scans.

Art of Darkness Modules

This section describes the ten modules that are included with this book.

Blackboard

Start with a clean slate, then let the Blackboard module scrawl on it. You never know what this one will come up with.

Blackboard is the handiwork of Mark Malamud and Susan Hautala of Seattle. This module writes on the screen with varying levels of neatness. Sliders let you set the sophistication of the writer (from Underachiever to Einstein), number of errors (set the error level high and you can practically taste the chalk dust from the eraser), neatness, and number of lines.

Mark and Susan worked many long hours on this module.

Mark, who used to reside on the East Coast, had to import special shipments of Yoo-Hoo chocolate drink and Mallomar cookies to get the job done.

> I did not see Elvis.
> I did not see elvis.
> I did not see elv

Bogglins

Are you tired of being labeled a member of America's cultural elite? Sure, you've tried to be just a regular guy or gal; you've taken to wearing bowling shirts to the office and surreptitiously reading your copy of *Being and Nothingness* behind a comic book. You've even given up using largish words like "surreptitiously," replacing them with more colloquial variants such as "sneaky-like." As a last resort, you've decorated your office with slogans such as "Work: The Curse of the Drinking Class!" and tapestries of canines playing cards. But to no avail! Your coworkers still have you pegged as a danged intellectual, and they resent you for being one.

Your troubles are over! Just fire up the Bogglins module and watch your popularity soar. Bogglins was written by Andy Karn, based on art submitted by Dann Auld to the 1992 After Dark Contest. A Bogglin, as the module's info screen explains, "is sort of a cross between Santa Claus and a pickle." The poor creature has apparently eaten something that doesn't agree with him, as evidenced by the sound effects (which you can, fortunately, turn down or off). Bogglins has only two sliders: Explosiveness, as you might expect, determines how quickly he explodes. The Twanginess slider, as its name implies, sets

how often he twangs, from Mild (hardly ever) to Sharp (frequently).

Helpful hint: This is probably not a good module to have activated during an important corporate presentation.

Fractal Forest

Fractal Forest was created by Scott Armitage, who got the idea for the module as he was looking out the window of his idyllic Minnesota home. As you've probably guessed, this module uses fractal geometry to create shapes that look like different types of trees. (For an introduction to fractals, see the earlier description of After Dark's Mandelbrot module.)

You can select the type of tree you want, or set the Type menu to Random for a variety of foliage. You can also set the number of trees (from 0 to 100) and the season (choose one of the fab four, or cycle through the seasons).

If you turn the sound on, you'll notice the cheerful chirping of birds during the spring, summer, and fall. I used ResEdit, the ornithologist's friend, to discover that the bird songs come from a thrush, a vireo, and a grosbeak (ResEdit is discussed in Chapter 4). In the spring and fall, you can see a flock of migrating birds. With their usual attention to scientific detail, Berkeley Systems has made sure the birds fly south in the winter and north in the spring (but only if your Mac is facing west).

If you're pining for Ma Nature, you might try combining Fractal Forest with Meadow, Mountains, Rainstorm, and/or Zot! in a MultiModule.

For a look at Fractal Forest's colorful foliage, see Plate 2.

Tip: If you're anywhere near your Mac around Christmastime, you might want to venture into the Fractal Forest.

Major Metaphysical Appliances

For reasons that are painfully obvious, I've nicknamed this module "Ohm Appliances." It was written by Gregory Becker, who works in a metaphysical bookstore in San Jose. Now, many people might be surprised that San Jose even has a

Disclaimers: Spin cycles are not subject to the Coriolis effect. Freezer contents may vary.

metaphysical bookstore. Somehow this farming community–cum–high-technology belt doesn't strike the casual observer as a metaphysical kind of town. But I live in San Jose, and I'm here to tell you that folks here wax metaphysical all the time. "Those fries are coming, sir," you're liable to hear, "just as soon as I finish pondering the transmigration of the soul." It's because we don't have our own baseball team, and there's not much else to do.

You can pretty much figure out this module's controls by fooling around with them, but I'll provide a few instructions for the unenlightened. The Entities slider lets you set the number of appliances (from 1 to 20). The Life Energy slider (measured in kilowatt hours) determines how quickly the refrigerators depart this mortal coil. The Defrost slider determines how often the refrigerators offer you a brief glimpse of inner peace (and/or frozen food). The Washer Karma slider determines how often a washing machine will insert itself into the Cosmic order.

Tip: Set the Defrost frequency high and the Washer Karma low to hear the maximum number of ohms.

For a look at some appliances, see Plate 3.

Movies 'Til Dawn

This module by Rob Vaterlaus lets you view QuickTime movies on your screen. QuickTime is Apple's new architecture for displaying not only static images, but sound, animation, and video on the Mac. An animation or digital video file in QuickTime format is called a QuickTime movie.

Note: Movies 'Til Dawn requires QuickTime to run.

You can get the QuickTime INIT by purchasing Apple's QuickTime Starter Kit; QuickTime is also included with Mac video-editing programs such as Adobe Premiere and DiVA VideoShop. The QuickTime Starter Kit includes numerous samples of QuickTime movies; you can also purchase floppy disks or CD ROMs filled with QuickTime movie clips, or get them from online services or user groups.

To use Movies 'Til Dawn, first make sure that QuickTime is installed in your Mac's System folder. Put all the QuickTime movies you want to display into a folder, and name it something like "Movies." Then, open the module and click the Pick Movie button. Locate your Movies folder and double-click its name to open it. If you want to play a single movie, click that movie's name, then click the Open button. If you want to cycle through all the movies in your Movies folder, check the Play All Movies In Folder option. (For variety, you might want to put groups of films in separate folders and select the folder you want for a double feature or film festival.)

In the Movies 'Til Dawn control panel, you can select where the movies will appear (in the center of your screen or at a new location each time) and in what order (alphabetical or random). If you want to see the name of a movie as it's playing, check the Show Name box. If your movie has sound, turn it up if you wish.

I like to combine Movies 'Til Dawn with Meadow in a MultiModule I call "Drive-In Movie." (Place Meadow in the back layer and a transparent Movies 'Til Dawn — with the Where option set to Center — in the middle of the screen.) Or, you might want to combine Movies 'Til Dawn with the Messages module to add subtitles to your films.

Pearls

Andy Karn of Berkeley Systems came up with this little gem. It uses fractal geometry (see the "Mandelbrot" section earlier in this chapter for a definition of fractals) to fill the screen with patterns made up of shapes within shapes within shapes. Pearls' pop-up menu lets you select the type of decorations — the shapes that are the basic design elements. Your choices are Tears, Tear Drops, Shiny Tears, Paper Tears, Neon Tears, Rays, Triangles, Neon Angles, Squares, Square Tiles, Octagons, and Octiles. Shiny Tears include highlights, Square Tiles and

Octiles have a 3-D appearance, and the Neon decorations are composed of colored tubes. (I love the term "Neon Tears." It sounds like it should be the name of a honky-tonk on the outskirts of Reno.)

Sliders let you set the display's detail and duration. The Detail slider ranges from fine to coarse. Set the Pause slider to the number of seconds you'd like each Pearls display to stay on the screen after the drawing cycle is complete (from 0 to 80 seconds).

See Plate 4 for a sample of what this module can do.

ProtoToasters

You are now the owner of an antique After Dark module. (In the computer world anything that's more than two years old is considered an antique. Unfortunately, most computer antiques, unlike their porcelain or wood counterparts, tend to go down in value as time progresses.)

ProtoToasters is Jack Eastman's original artwork for what later became After Dark's Flying Toasters module. (A small minority at Berkeley Systems lobbied for using this artwork in After Dark, but Nick Rush, a man of high aesthetic ideals, persuaded the company to hire a professional artist.)

See Chapter 2 for details on the history of this flying appliance.

ProtoToasters fly skillfully, despite their stubby wings.

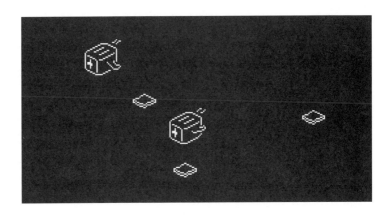

Spin Brush

Brian Lowry, who also wrote the Terraform module, came up with this artistic screen saver. Spin Brush smears the contents of the screen like a wet brush on paper. You can set the Spin type to Spin, Spiral, Star, or Stretch, or alternate between them with the Mixed setting.

The Switch Every slider lets you set how often the module switches the point the brush spins around (and the type of brush, if Mixed is selected). Another slider lets you set the brush thickness, while a checkbox gives you the option of smearing what's on the screen or starting with a preset background pattern.

Tip: For best results on a color monitor, make sure there's something colorful on your screen for Spin Brush to paint on.

You can achieve some striking effects by combining Brian's two modules in Randomizer. Although Randomizer usually displays modules one after another, with the right settings you can make two modules overlap.

1. Set Spin Brush to Switch every 1 minute, with a brush thickness of 4 and the Spin type set to Spin.

2. Pick a colorful Terraform terrain such as Tropical, Forest, or Neon. Set Land to Random, Water to Islands, and Clouds to Wispy. Set the Repeat Size to 256 and the Idle Time to 60 seconds. (You can come up with your own settings for each module, but this recipe is a good starting point.)

3. In Randomizer, set the Order to Random and the Duration to 30 seconds.

4. Run Randomizer and watch what happens.

For a look at Spin Brush in action, see Plate 5.

Strange Attractors

This module, by Ed Hall, is named after a term found in physics. *Strange attractors* is a term coined by David Ruelle and Floris Talkens, two scientists who were studying fluid dynamics in the 1960s and '70s. They were studying the phenomenon of turbulence, trying to discern the complex interplay of forces that make a smoothly flowing stream break into a tangled jumble of eddies, whirlpools, and ripples. Strange attractors exist in *phase space,* a system that allows scientists to represent numerical data as pictures, tracing the progress of a dynamic process — represented as a single point — through space and time. (Who said this wasn't an educational book?)

Strange attractors are but one aspect of the theory of chaos, a fledgling science that has become popular of late. (If you want more information on the theory of chaos, I'd suggest the book *Chaos: Making a New Science,* by James Gleick [Viking 1987]). I have been studying chaos for years, in my own modest way, observing in my office the complex workings of a system I call *paper dynamics.* Paper dynamics tries to find an underlying pattern in the distribution of books, magazines, press releases, correspondence, and so forth, as they develop into larger and larger stacks. I've observed some interesting phenomena in my studies: for example, a pile of software manuals in one corner has grown so dense over the years that I'm relatively sure it's compressed itself into a miniature black hole. I'm certain that I saw it suck in the cat last week. Although I can't claim to fully understand the workings of paper dynamics, I believe I've discovered the force that causes the chaos to happen: *me.* I hope that in the near future scientists will endeavor to discover how I affect other systems, such as sock disappearance and refrigerator life-forms. If any scientists out there are interested in studying me, please contact me in care of my publisher.

But I digress. Again. Sorry. Although they're derived from

mathematical formulas, the strange attractors you'll see in After Dark look oddly organic. If you free-associate, you're likely to see all sorts of strange things: bird skulls, cross-sections of arterial walls, magnified diatoms, Ukrainian Easter-egg patterns, jeweled brooches, carnival masks, lace doilies, aboriginal art, or monsters from the Id.

Strange Attractors is, in my opinion, the most beautiful After Dark module of them all.

See Plate 6 for a sample of Strange Attractors.

SunBurst

This module is by Jean Tantra, who also wrote Stained Glass (Stained Glass was described in the "More After Dark" section of this book. Like Stained Glass, SunBurst was inspired by the art of quilting; *sunburst* is the name of a quilting pattern.

Sunburst displays a swirling array of patterns that might remind you of a kaleidoscope. The slider controls how quickly a new SunBurst pattern will appear on the screen.

For a SunBurst sample, see Plate 7.

After Dark Updater

The After Dark Updater that's on the Art of Darkness disk isn't a module; it's a utility that updates your After Dark application and modules if necessary. The utility updates older versions of After Dark (2.0, 2.0h, 2.0s, 2.0t, and 2.0u) to the newer version 2.0v, which is compatible with the newer, 68040-processor-based Macs. If you're not sure which version of After Dark (or which Mac processor chip) you have, it's OK to run the Updater. If your version of After Dark is up to date, the Updater will let you know.

Note: This utility is also included on the More After Dark disk. If you've already updated your copy of After Dark with that utility, you don't need to use the version included with this book.

To run the After Dark Updater, perform these steps:

1. Copy the After Dark Updater Utility from the Art of Darkness disk to your hard disk.

2. Make sure After Dark is in the proper location on your hard disk: if you're running System 6, After Dark and the After Dark Files folder should be in the System folder; if you're running System 7, After Dark should be in the Control Panels or Extensions folder, and the After Dark Files folder should be in the System folder, Control Panels folder, or Extensions folder, or on the desktop.

3. Double-click the After Dark Updater icon.

4. Choose Update from the File menu. The utility will update your After Dark program and modules if necessary.

5. Quit the Updater.

6. Restart your Mac to run the updated After Dark.

Public Domain and Shareware Modules

If your appetite for After Dark modules isn't satisfied by After Dark, More After Dark, and the ten modules that come with this book, you can always download additional modules from online bulletin boards like CompuServe or America Online or purchase a disk of them from your local user group. The following is a sampling of some of the public-domain (free) and shareware (cheap) modules you can find.

Note: Modules posted on bulletin boards don't necessarily have the blessings of Berkeley Systems. So, if you download modules from an online service, please don't (1) pester Berkeley Systems' tech support staff with questions, or (2) blame Berkeley Systems if your shareware or public-domain module crashes or otherwise misbehaves. Thanks.

Invert

This $5 shareware module by Richard Lesh simply inverts the screen, starting at the outer edges and working its way in. Combine it with other modules in MultiModule for some interesting effects.

Off the Air

This one's bound to stymie your officemates. Off the Air makes your Mac act like a TV set that's left on after a station's signed off. The screen is filled with static and snow, and a realistic hissing sound is included.

This shareware module by Guy T. Rice can be yours for only $2. (As an incentive to get you to send in your two bucks, the author promises to make a future version display the American flag and play the National Anthem before going off the air — financial resources permitting.)

Note: This module requires a setting of 256 colors or grays.

Spill

In this free module by Dominic Mazzoni, a wall of black goo seeps down your screen. You can set the Number of Drips from 1 (a simple black curtain descends) to 20 (looks like runny paint or tar).

Spinning Bow Tie

This free module by Steven Loomis is based on the Bouncing Ball code that's provided for programmers on the After Dark disk. In this case, it's a bow tie shape that bounces around the screen, twirling around and leaving beautiful trails of color as it moves. Sliders allow you to control the speed and size of the traveling tie.

Swarm!

Computerized bees! What won't they think of next? This free screen saver by Dan Walkowski and Johnny Zweig places a frenetic swarm of bees on your screen. Sliders let you set the number of bees (from Few to Jillions), Jiggle Factor (how rigorously the swarm stays in formation), the Queen Speed (from Slow to Frantic), and the Drone Speed (also from Slow to Frantic). The drones will do their best to follow the queen as she swoops and darts around the screen.

You can spoil the mood of Meadow by adding a swarm of bees in MultiModule, or combine Swarm! with Can of Worms and the butterfly from Boris for an entomological treat.

Now that you've gotten a taste of what these modules can do, it's time to start combining them with MultiModule to produce even more impressive effects.

69

CHAPTER 3

Multi Module Cookbook

MultiModule Cookbook

No aspect of After Dark is more fun — and less utilized — than the versatile MultiModule. I know, I know…many of you are busy executives who don't have time to fool with customizing a screen saver. But let's look at this from a cost-effectiveness standpoint. With MultiModule, you could easily double the number of screen savers on your computer — without paying a cent. And with the recipes presented in this chapter (and, I hope, the ideas they'll inspire), you'll be able to make custom modules that are so ingenious that your colleagues won't be able to tell they originated in After Dark.

What Is a MultiModule?

In case you've never created a MultiModule, here's a brief description. MultiModule is itself an After Dark module that lets you combine two or more After Dark modules into a new one, which can then be accessed like any other module.

Each module in a MultiModule can be placed in its own separate location on the screen (you might divide the screen into quarters, for example, with a module in each section), or modules can overlap for interesting effects.

To create a new MultiModule, select MultiModule from the After Dark control panel, then click the New button. The following window appears:

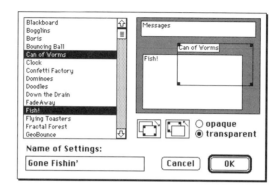

Select the first module for your new creation from the scrolling list on the left. A rectangle representing the module will appear in the MultiModule window, which represents your Mac's screen. Black handles at the corners of the module rectangle allow you to stretch or shrink it. If you wish, you can resize the module so it fills the entire screen. You can move modules around on the screen as well; place the arrow cursor in the center of the module rectangle to drag the module to any position on the screen.

Next, choose a second module from the scrolling list. You'll notice that both the modules you've selected remain highlighted in the list to remind you which ones you've chosen (believe me, they can get lost in the Mac-screen window once you start stacking them up). The second module is automatically layered on top of the first. Position the second module where you want it.

Since the second module is stacked on top of the first, it will cover up part of the first module if they overlap. You can solve this problem in a couple of ways. The simplest, of course, is to move the second module's rectangle so it doesn't touch the first module's. That's fine, unless you want the modules to interact. Another solution is to click on the second module to select it (the black handles will appear when it's selected), then click the Transparent button. This button makes the module's black background transparent, so the first module shows through (the module's name is surrounded by a box when the Transparent setting is chosen). *Tip: Select and drag transparent modules by clicking on the name box.* In most cases, you'll probably want to make most or all of your MultiModule components transparent, but a few exceptions exist (these are discussed later in this chapter).

Once you've placed a series of modules in the MultiModule window, name your new module in the Name of Settings box and click the OK button. You'll return to the MultiModule control panel. To test your MultiModule, click the Demo button, or — to see a full-screen version without the control panel in the way — place the cursor in the sleep corner you've specified in After Dark's setup dialog box (accessed by pressing the When button).

Chances are your MultiModule won't behave perfectly the first time you test it. A common problem on color monitors is color distortion; one of the modules might display garish colors, for example, rather than its normal colors (see the "Off-Color Toasters" example below for a solution). Or perhaps you forgot to set a certain attribute, such as speed or number of objects, in one of the original modules. Or maybe you put in a module that just doesn't look as good as you thought it would in that particular MultiModule. Not to worry. You can edit the MultiModule.

Return to the MultiModule control panel and click the Edit button. You'll see the setup window for your MultiModule. You can fool with the MultiModule as much as you like. You may need to make a module transparent or opaque (select the module and click the appropriate button), shift it in front of or behind another module (select the module and click one of the icons that indicates move forward or move backward), delete it (select the module and press the Delete key on the Mac's keyboard), resize it (drag the rectangle's handles), or change its position on the screen (drag from the center of the rectangle). In some cases, you'll need to revise the settings in a module itself. To do so, click on the module's name in the scrolling list, select the settings you want, then click MultiModule in the scrolling list and continue working on the MultiModule.

In many cases you'll have to tweak a MultiModule several times before you get the effect you want, but the results are usually worth the trouble. When you're done, click OK, and the name of your new MultiModule is added to the pop-up menu at the top of the MultiModule control panel. Place the cursor on this menu and hold down the mouse button to view the menu and select other MultiModules.

MultiModule 101

Now that you know the basics of MultiModules, you're ready to make your own. After Dark comes with several sample MultiModules (look in the MultiModules pop-up menu), but, frankly, you can do better than those. Let's start with a simple MultiModule that involves two After Dark modules, Message and Zot!.

I Mean It!

To add some oomph to a message on your screen, you can use MultiModule to add a few lightning bolts.

First, open the Messages module and click the Edit Message button. In the dialog box that appears, type your own message — maybe something like "Back in a flash!" for when you vacate your desk for a bit. Set the font, style, color, and size you want, then click OK. Select Popping from the Move menu (this option will cause your message to pop up at various locations on the screen) and set the Speed slider to Spritely. Turn the sound off.

Next, choose the Zot! module. Choose whatever slider settings you'd like, and turn the sound up to medium or loud.

Open a new MultiModule and select Messages. Drag the rectangle's handles until it fills the entire screen. Then, select Zot! and do the same. With the Zot! rectangle still selected, click the Transparent button.

Click OK, then click the Demo button. A pretty emphatic message will appear on your screen.

That's all there is to it. Before you start making your own MultiModules, it would behoove you to read the following tips and caveats. Then you'll be ready to try out some of the recipes in this chapter, or dive right in and invent some custom MultiModules.

Fixing a Fundamental Flaw

(Good old alliteration, the hack writer's best friend! Actually it's the computer writer's second-best friend, right after the car analogy. But I digress.)

MultiModules, wonderful as they are, have an irritating flaw. Modules, as you know, have their own settings: the darkness of the toast in Flying Toasters, for example, or the number of cats in Boris. When you create a MultiModule out of two or more modules, how the MultiModule performs depends on the settings in each module it contains. If these settings are changed within the original module, the MultiModule will behave differently, reflecting the most recent settings of each module it contains. This feature can be very annoying, since you must either refrain from changing the properties of any modules that are included in MultiModules, or tweak the settings of individual modules when you want to run a MultiModule that contains them.

Not to worry; there's an easy way around this problem. All you have to do is use *copies* of modules in your MultiModules; that way, you can have one group of settings for the regular version of a module, and another for the version of that module that's used in a MultiModule. Let's say, for example, that you want to combine Boris and Rain in a MultiModule. Here's what you do:

1. Open your After Dark Files folder, the folder that contains all the modules.

2. Click on the Boris module (name or icon, depending on how you've chosen to display the files in this folder) to select it.

3. Choose Duplicate from the File menu (or press ⌘-D as a shortcut). This creates a duplicate of the selected file.

4. The Duplicate command creates a twin file called "Boris copy." You can rename the file if you wish; you might want to choose a name that relates to the MultiModule you're building. For this example, we'll call the new file "Soaking Kitty."

5. Duplicate and rename any other modules you want to put in your MultiModule. In this case, you could create a duplicate called "Soaking Rain." (Renaming the files in this way has the advantage of placing them next to each other in After Dark's alphabetical module list, saving you precious seconds that might otherwise be spent scrolling through the list when you construct the MultiModule).

   You can make as many duplicate modules as you wish, saving custom settings for multiple MultiModules — or simply for different solo performances of your favorite module.

6. Use the duplicated files to construct a MultiModule. The settings you've selected in the duplicates will be applied when the MultiModule runs.

Sound Advice

Many After Dark modules include sound. You can turn it up, down, or off, depending on your preferences (and those of the people around you). Although you can combine several sounds in a MultiModule, they may fight with each other if two or more try to play at once, producing a cacophony of sounds that are cut short by one another. In general, it's a good idea to turn up the sound for only one or two modules in a MultiModule.

Note: Multi-Module's sound setting controls the volume for the overall Multi-Module. In other words, even if you have the volume set low for the individual modules that comprise your MultiModule, the volume will be played high if the MultiModule sound control is set to high.

You can use MultiModule to add sound to an otherwise mute module. To do so, open a new MultiModule and select the module whose sound you want to use (make sure the sound is turned up in the module). Place that module into the MultiModule. Next, select the soundless module and place it in the MultiModule (it will be stacked on top of the first module). Drag the second module's rectangle so it completely covers the first one, and make sure the second module is set to Opaque. Since the second module obscures the first one, you'll see only the second one when you run the MultiModule, but hear the sounds from the module that's lurking underneath. As an example, you might want to place Nocturnes beneath Meadow to produce a meadow full of chirping crickets (and the occasional howling wolf). You can also use this trick to change the sound in an existing module that includes sound. Just turn off the sound in the module you wish to view, and follow the procedure just described to place an invisible, sound-playing module behind it.

MultiModules on the Menu

All the MultiModules you create are displayed in the Multi-Module control panel's pop-up menu. If you want to run a particular MultiModule, just select it from the pop-up menu's list. If you create a MultiModule that you use all the time, you can place its name in After Dark's scrolling list, just as if it were a regular module. To place a MultiModule in After Dark's module list, perform the following procedure:

1. Create a MultiModule and name it, as usual, in MultiModule's module-creation window. (Or select a MultiModule you've already created from MultiModule's pop-up menu.)

2 Quit After Dark.

3. Open the System folder, find the After Dark Files folder, and open it.

4. Click on the MultiModule icon and make a duplicate (select Duplicate from the File menu or press ⌘-D). Give the duplicate a name that describes your new MultiModule.

5. When you reopen After Dark, you'll see your new Multi-Module in the scrolling list of module names.

Now you can select your favorite MultiModules from After Dark's scrolling module list, instead of having to open Multi-Module and select them from that module's pop-up menu.

MultiModule Safety Tip

I'm not trying to scare you here, so read the following tip in the soothing and cheery tones of a flight attendant making the obligatory "In the unlikely event of a water landing…" spiel.

Although it's not likely to happen to you, I feel it's my duty to warn you that I've occasionally crashed my Mac when creating a MultiModule. Certain modules in certain combinations just don't seem to get along. Therefore, before you make a MultiModule (especially if you're using public-domain or shareware modules, which haven't been tested by Berkeley Systems), make sure all the files you're working on are saved.

MultiModule Recipes

This section presents numerous recipes — in no particular order — for creating interesting or whimsical MultiModules. Unless otherwise noted, all modules in a MultiModule should be enlarged to fill the entire screen. Also, in most cases the module in the back layer (the first module you select in Multi-Module) should be opaque, and those on top of it transparent.

Butterfly Meadow

This charming MultiModule is made up of only two modules from More After Dark, Meadow and Boris.

1. In the Meadow module (or a copy thereof), set the Starting Season to Summer and the Seasons Last slider to Forever.

2. In Boris, set the Number of Cats to 0 (something I wish I could do in real life around here on many a meow-filled morning) and the Butterfly slider to Always. Turn off the sound (unless you want a butterfly that meows and purrs).

3. In MultiModule, select Meadow and enlarge it to fill the entire screen. Then select Boris, resize it to fill the whole screen, and click the Transparent button.

You'll now have a lovely butterfly flitting about in a field of flowers.

Boris Follies

The following modules make use of good old Boris the cat, who's great to use in MultiModules because — unlike the occupants of most other modules — he isn't surrounded by a black rectangle that erases whatever he passes. (Plus, he's cute as the dickens.)

(Note: Some twisted individuals have been known to combine Boris the cat with Mowin' Man in a MultiModule, but you wouldn't do something that gross, would you, gentle reader?)

Cat on the Desktop This MultiModule is likely to make your officemates do a double-take when they pass your Mac.

1. Use the ⌘-Shift-3 key combination (or a screen-capture utility such as Capture) to make a screen shot of your Mac's desktop. The file will be named Picture 0 (or some other number if you've taken previous screen shots). You can rename the picture if you wish.

2. Place this picture in the Picture Frame module, and select it with the Choose Picture button. Set the intensity to 100%. (This won't make for a very effective screen saver, but this MultiModule is meant to be cute, not functional.)

3. In the Boris module, set the Number of Cats to 1 and the Butterfly setting to Never. Turn up the sound if you wish.

4. In MultiModule, choose Picture Frame and resize it to fill the entire screen. Then select Boris and resize the rectangle to fill the entire screen as well. Make the Boris module transparent.

When this module comes on, a little cat will scamper across what appears to be your desktop.

Boris at Play If you want to give Boris something to amuse him, combine the Boris module with a bouncing ball or two from Gravity and a small chunk of string from String Theory.

Moon Kitty Since Boris often scampers diagonally across the screen, he works quite well in the craggy landscapes of the Mountains module. Place Mountains in the background, and a transparent Boris on top.

Confetti Kitty Combine Boris with Confetti Factory for an amusing MultiModule. He doesn't seem to faze the ducks a bit.

Cat-o-Matic Combine Boris with Puzzle for a unique display. Watch Boris try to navigate his way around an endless series of slamming cat doors.

Off-Color Toasters

If you've ever combined Flying Toasters in a MultiModule with certain other modules, you may have noticed that the toast and toasters sometimes take on psychedelic hues. This is because certain modules — including Toasters — use their own *color palette,* a collection of colors specific to that module. Try, for example, creating a MultiModule by placing Flying Toasters, then Boris, in the MultiModule window. The toasters will look somewhat like the t-shirts worn by the audience at a Grateful Dead concert. Why? Because the color palette of the frontmost item in a MultiModule (Boris, in this case) takes precedence over other palettes.

Don't worry; you can fix it. If you want the toasters to retain their lovely brown-and-chrome color scheme, here's what you do:

1. In the MultiModule window, select the Edit button.

2. Click on the Flying Toasters rectangle to select it, then click the Frontward icon to bring Toasters to the front.

Now, when you run the MultiModule, the toasters will have their original colors.

Grateful Toast

Of course, some people might actually *want* psychedelic toasters. Perhaps they remind you of the glorious Sixties (not you, Mr. X). For optimum psychedelia, place Satori behind some opaque Flying Toasters in a MultiModule.

Tip: The Satori module creates some interesting effects with other After Dark modules as well. Open MultiModule and experiment with the Satori effect. The same applies to the Vertigo module, which produces some bizarre color changes itself.

Toast Rectangles

Fun Physics Fact #2: Each toaster exists in a black rectangle. This doesn't matter when the toasters are simply flying around in their home environment, since the background is black and toasters aren't allowed to overlap one another. But it can be annoying in MultiModules, when the rectangles blot out surrounding graphics. There's nothing you can do to get rid of the rectangles, but you can minimize their unsightly appearance by combining Toasters with other modules that have black backgrounds (look at the "Space Toasters" example in MultiModule, for example) and/or combining them with a minimal number of objects from other modules. One of my favorite toast-related MultiModules is one I call Butter-Toast, which combines the flitting butterfly from Boris (in the Boris module, turn down the number of cats to 0) with a screenful of toast and toasters.

Clockwork Vertigo

This dizzying MultiModule idea was presented by Multi-Module Queen Cathy Abes.

1. Set the Clock module to Type: Modern, Sound: None, and Float Speed: Normal.

2 Make a copy of the Clock module and leave the settings

the same, except for setting the clock type to Antique.

3. In Vertigo, set Shapes to Spirals or Zooms, Spiral Pitch to 90, Color Speed to 300, and Idle Time to 5.

4. Make two more copies of Vertigo, changing the settings as you wish.

5. Stack up the modules, making them all full-screen-sized and transparent.

The result is a colorful display of kinetic art (see Plate 8).

Calling All Sickos!

The following modules can be viewed as educational animations depicting the plight of our environment. Or, they can be seen as disgusting perversions of the MultiModule concept. Take your pick.

Compost Heap Use the method described earlier (the "Cat On the Desktop" example under "Boris Follies") to make a fake desktop in Picture Frame. Then, in MultiModule, put the desktop in the back layer and place a postage-stamp-sized rectangle of Meadow (set to Summer, Forever) right about where the Mac's trash can is on the desktop. Voilà! Flowers bloom around the trash can. Sometimes this configuration will produce little random dots above the flowers which, with a little imagination, could pass for flies.

Strip Mining Set Terraform to a Repeat Size of 256 and an Idle Time of 20 seconds. Set the module's Terrain to Moon or Tundra, Land to Random, Water to Highlands, and Clouds to Clear.

Set Mowin' Man to Hurried, Mow Every 3 Days, Growth Rate: None, and sound on.

Place Terraform in the background, and a transparent Mowin' Man in front. You'll get the picture.

Acid Rainfall Place Fractal Forest (10 or 20 trees, any season but winter) in the background. Place a transparent Rain module in the foreground. Ugh! The rain eats the leaves right off the trees.

Author's disclaimer: Hey! Lighten up. I'm a longtime member of many fine ecological organizations. I'm just warped.

Staintory

In Stained Glass, set Complexity to 0, Duplication to 50, and Color to 100. Fill the MultiModule window with Stained Glass. Place a small square of Satori in the center of the screen, on top of the Stained Glass. (Both modules should be opaque.)

Have patience. This one will take a little time to draw the initial image.

Bouncin' Bogglins

Combine our flatulent friend from the Art of Darkness disk with a few colorful balls from Gravity for a festive display.

Newton

Make three copies of the Globe module, each with slightly different settings for Rotation and Shadow.

In MultiModule, set the Globes to Transparent and position them so they overlap somewhat. You'll have your own planetary system on the screen..

For a more elaborate MultiModule, you might want to place your planets on top of Warp!, or place different surfaces on a Globe or two (use ⌘-Shift-3 to capture some terrain from Terraform, then map it onto your Globe with the module's Image controls).

(See the "Stars and Asteroids" section later in this chapter for a tip on how to add more heavenly bodies to your display.)

NBA

If they won't let you watch basketball games on TV at your place of employment, you can always fantasize by running this MultiModule.

1. In the Gravity module, set the Number of Balls to 1 and the Diameter to Big. Turn off the Leave Trails option.

2. In String Art, set the Delay to 10 seconds, Number of Lines to 50, and Color Cycles to 1. Then make a copy of String Art.

3. In MultiModule, place a small square of String Art on one side of your screen, and a square of the same size (the copy of String Art you made earlier) on the opposite side. Then place a transparent, full-screen version of Gravity on top of the two String Art squares.

Well, it's better than no basketball at all.

Saint Patrick

Combine Puzzle and Snake in a MultiModule (Puzzle set to Transparent, in the top layer), and watch the poor snake's confusion as it tries to escape.

Satorp!

To see the underlying structure of the Universe, combine Warp! and Satori. (Warp! should be set to Transparent and placed in the top layer of the MultiModule.) Whew!

Mandelic

For a stunning display, place Satori (Opaque) in the bottom layer of a MultiModule, then Mandelbrot (also Opaque) in the front layer.

Stars and Asteroids

Using this hitherto-unknown technique, you can add floating asteroids and spaceships to most any After Dark module. (See Chapter 2 for a detailed description of the Logo module.)

1. Start up the Lunatic Fringe module.

2. Press the Caps Lock key to display the Lunatic Fringe Bestiary. Keeping the Caps Lock key held down, simultaneously press the ⌘, Shift, and 3 keys (the combo that takes a screen shot).

3. Find the file called "Picture 0" and open it, either with a graphics program that lets you open PICT files, or with Apple's TeachText program.

4. Select a spaceship, asteroid, or other object from the Lunatic Fringe picture, either with your graphics program's selection tool or TeachText's crosshair cursor.

5. Choose Copy from the Edit menu (or use the ⌘-C shortcut) to copy the object to the Clipboard.

6. Open the Logo module and click the Pictures button. In the dialog box that appears, click the Paste button. Your space graphic will appear in Logo's picture window, ready to use with the Logo module. Click OK.

7. Create a MultiModule with a module of your choice in the background. For example, you might use Starry Skyline as the background module, placing a transparent Logo module containing an asteroid over the top half of the screen. Or, you might want to use this technique to place a flying spaceship in the Warp! module. Better yet, you might want to place two or more spaceships in another module. Simply make one or more copies of Logo, each with a different object.

Hint: Use different float speeds in Logo and different screen positions for each Logo in Multi-Module for best results.

Rain of Terror

Here's an easy one. Place Nocturnes in the background, and overlay a transparent Rain. Keep the sound on for both modules.

Muybridge

This MultiModule is reminiscent (well, sort of) of the motion-study photos of Eadweard Muybridge, who began his unique style of photography to settle a bet on whether all four feet of a trotting horse are ever off the ground simultaneously (they are). Muybridge rigged up an elaborate series of trip-wires and cameras to take series of photos of humans and animals in motion. Now you can perform similar tests on Boris the cat (do all his paws ever leave the ground at the same time?).

In Boris, set the Number of Cats to 3 and Butterfly to Never. In Stained Glass, set Complexity to 0, Duplication to 50, and Color to 100.

Place Stained Glass (opaque, full-screen) in the MultiModule window, then place a small patch of Boris (about 2 inches squre, also opaque) in the center of the screen.

When you run this MultiModule, you should see cats appearing in numerous frames on your screen.

Wild Planet

Place Mountains in the background, then add a transparent Zot! in the foreground. This module simulates the tempestuous birth of a new planet.

Author's note: One afternoon during the last week of this project, I was taking a little break and looking out my back window. I have a large swatch of California poppies in my back yard, and I watched as a couple of butterflies fluttered by. Then my gray-and-white cat wandered onto the scene. Know what I said to myself? "This looks like a MultiModule." A sure sign that I've been working too hard!

Advanced
Module
Modification

Major Metaphysical Appliances

```
0101 1101      0101 1101      0101 1101
0010 1001      0010 1001      0010 1001
0110 1010      0110 1010      0110 1010
0001 1110      0001 1110      0001 1110
0100 0000      0100 0000      0100 0000
...            ...            ...
```
ADgm   ADrk   Chn1   PICT   snd

```
               0101 1101      0101 1101      The
               0010 1001      0010 1001      *quick*
               0110 1010      0110 1010      **brown**
               0001 1110      0001 1110      ...
               0100 0000      0100 0000
               ...            ...
```

Advanced Module Modification

This chapter is for those of you who want to push the envelope of screen saver customization. (Well, we must push our envelopes where we can; we can't all be jet pilots and arctic explorers now, can we?) If you want to get your hands dirty and get in there and modify the very pictures and sounds that make up a module, then read on. (A few of these tips require Apple's ResEdit utility.)

Customizing After Dark

The following tips show you how to customize After Dark in a number of ways, from reordering the list of modules to altering a module's graphics and sound.

A New Module Order

Are you tired of scrolling through a lengthy list of modules in After Dark's control panel? You have several options for providing quick access to your favorite modules.

- The easiest method for speedy list navigation is to type the first few letters of a module's name. This will automatically select the module (or at least a nearby module that starts with the same few letters).

- If even typing a few letters is too tedious for you, you might want to streamline your After Dark menu by deleting modules you never use. Open the After Dark Files folder and throw away the modules you don't want (make sure you have the originals somewhere, in case you want to reinstall them sometime), or put them in another folder for storage (name the folder anything except "After Dark Files.").

- If neither of the above methods suits you, you might try bringing your favorite modules to the top of the After Dark module list. The Mac has a somewhat broader view of alphabetization than you or I do, and has a whole series of characters that it lists before the letters of our puny human alphabet. The easiest to remember are numbers (computers start counting at 0, remember), but the following characters fall even before numbers in the computer alphabet:

  ! # $ % & * ( ) @ ^

The astute reader will notice that these characters correspond to the letters you get when you press the Shift key and type the number keys. The even astuter reader will notice that the @ and ^ characters seem to be out of order in this list, since they appear on the 2 and 6 keys, respectively. Well, that's true. Don't ask me why; ask the guys who came up with the American Standard Code for Information Interchange. I'm sure they had a good reason for choosing the character order they came up with.

Anyway, you can use your reordered module list not only for easy access, but also to put modules in the proper order for display by the Slide Show or Randomizer modules. For example, you might want to display Satori, then Boris, then Ripple in Randomizer. Just rename these modules "1Satori,"

"2Boris," and "3Ripple," and they'll appear in the order you want.

Note: If After Dark is open while you're renaming modules, you must close it and reopen it in order for the modules to show up in the new order you've specified.

From Silent Modules to Talkies

As you've probably noticed, a number of After Dark modules don't include sound. The last chapter showed you how to add sound to mute modules by placing a sound-playing module behind another one in MultiModule. But that technique limits you to the sounds that come with the modules. If you have access to Apple's QuickTime and some QuickTime movie clips, you can add other sounds to your After Dark modules. (For a description of QuickTime, see the section on the Movies 'Til Dawn module in Chapter 2.)

1. Open the Movies 'Til Dawn module that comes with this book.

2. Click the Pick Movie button and select a QuickTime movie that has a soundtrack you'd like to use. Click on the movie's name to select it. (Make sure the Play All Movies in Folder option is *not* checked.) Click Open to return to After Dark's control panel.

3. In the Movies 'Til Dawn control panel, set the Where option to Center and the sound to the level you want. Click the Demo button to test the sound level.

4. Open a new MultiModule and place Movies 'Til Dawn in the back layer.

5. Place a soundless After Dark module, set to Opaque, on top of the Movies 'Til Dawn module.

Now, when you run the MultiModule, the sound from the QuickTime movie will accompany the module you selected. You could use this trick to add sound effects to modules such as Globe or Logo, or perhaps to add a musical fanfare to Spotlight. You could also turn off the sound in a sound-equipped module and use this technique to insert a different sound.

Random MultiModules

If you like to watch your favorite MultiModules over and over, you can play them with Randomizer, just as you would any other modules. Here's how.

1. Create a new MultiModule or select an existing one from MultiModule's pop-up menu. (If you're not familiar with MultiModules, see Chapter 3.)

2. Open the After Dark Files folder and click on MultiModule to select it. Select Duplicate from the File menu or press ⌘-D. This makes a copy of the currently selected MultiModule, and automatically names it "MultiModule copy."

3. Rename the "MultiModule copy" file. Pick a name that describes the selected MultiModule.

The next time you open After Dark, the MultiModule you just named will appear in After Dark's scrolling list. You can then select it from the list like any other module, and either run it directly from After Dark or place it in a Randomizer set.

Speed Up Your Modules

Sometimes After Dark modules run more slowly than usual. The following tips can help you speed up After Dark's performance.

- If a module seems to be running slowly, it may be slowing down so as not to interfere with other Macintosh processing activity. If you've checked the System IQ Activity Monitor option (accessed by clicking After Dark's When button), After Dark will monitor system activity and cut back if necessary. This is a normal part of After Dark's operation. Remember, After Dark is, beneath its glamorous exterior, a utility; it's not supposed to interfere with other programs.

- Running modules when a Microsoft Word document is open sure slows 'em down. For speedier module display, try turning off Word's Background Repagination option.

- If you're running an After Dark module for aesthetic reasons rather than utilitarian ones, you'll get slightly better performance if you close all your applications and documents.

Major Modifications

If you've made it to this point in the book, you're either an adventurous soul or someone with copious amounts of leisure time. Perhaps both. If you find that even MultiModule doesn't give you enough control over customizing After Dark, you might want to alter the graphics and sounds that make up some of After Dark's modules. You can do so with ResEdit, Apple's resource editor (a *resource* is a component of a program such as sound, text, or graphics). ResEdit allows people who don't know a lick of programming to go in and alter Mac programs. (If you want to learn more about ResEdit, I'd suggest that you purchase a book such as *ResEdit Complete,* by Peter Alley and Carolyn Strange (Addison-Wesley, 1991) or *Zen and the Art of Resource Editing,* edited by Derrick Schneider, Hans Hansen, and Noah Potkin (Peachpit Press, 1992). In addition to providing tips for using ResEdit, both of these books come with a copy of the ResEdit utility. If you don't want to buy a book, you can get hold of a copy of ResEdit from an online service or user group.

Warning: The usual ResEdit caveats are in order, although the current version of ResEdit doesn't fry files nearly as often as early versions did. First, always work on a backup copy of a file; if you do something wrong, you may not be able to recover the file you were messing with. Don't go gallivanting off into ResEdit and modifying other parts of the Flying Toasters module — especially if you don't know what you're doing. If you don't heed this warning, don't blame me if you toast your toasters — or some other file on your Mac.

Toast Your Own

In this example we'll use ResEdit to add a pat of butter (or margarine, if you prefer) to the toast that sails along with After Dark's Flying Toasters.

A word to the nice: Although it's OK for you to edit copies of After Dark modules for your own use, you should refrain from posting your handiwork on online bulletin boards. After all, what you're distributing is a slightly modified version of a program that Jack, Patrick, et al., worked hard to create. Think how you'd feel if someone changed a few lines of a book you'd written, then distributed it for free. All right, end of lecture.

Follow the steps below to customize your toast.

1. The first thing you should do is make a copy of the Flying Toasters module to work on. Open the After Dark Files folder and click on Flying Toasters. Select Duplicate from the File menu; the Mac will create a file called "Flying Toasters copy." Use this file with ResEdit.

2. Start up ResEdit.

3. In the dialog box that appears, double-click on "Flying

Toasters copy" to open the module in ResEdit.

4. A selection of icons will appear. Double-click the one labeled "PICT" (for picture file).

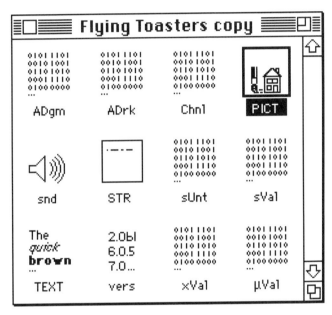

5. A large window will appear, depicting the four toasters that make up the Flying Toasters animation. You should see a series of black-and-white toasters and their complementary piece of toast, and — if you have a color monitor — color toasters and toast as well (on a monochrome monitor, the would-be color toasters will show up as black-and-white shadows of their color selves). Use the window's scroll bar to locate the piece of toast; we'll use the black-and-white toast in this example.

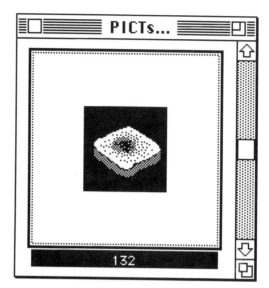

6. Next, select Copy from the Edit menu to copy the toast.

7. Quit ResEdit.

8. Open a paint program and select Paste from the Edit menu. The toast you just copied will appear. Use your paint program's tools to draw a dollop of butter, then place it on the toast (I've always wanted to use the word *dollop* in a computer book; you'd be surprised at how infrequently the opportunity arises). *Note: Don't change the size of the black rectangle that the toast resides in. If you do, the module won't work.*

9. Use your paint program's lasso tool to select the buttered toast, then choose Copy from the Edit menu.

10. Save your document, quit the paint program, and reopen ResEdit.

11. Repeat the first few steps to get to the ResEdit window that shows all the toasters. Click on the piece of toast, then choose Clear from the Edit menu (or press the Delete key).

12. Select Create New Resource from the Resource menu. A window labeled PICT ID will appear.

13. Select Paste from the Edit menu, and your edited toast will appear in the PICT ID window.

14. Close the window, and you'll see that your new toast has replaced the original one in the ResEdit window.

15. Quit ResEdit and rename your new Toasters module. Place the new module in the After Dark Files folder (if it's not already there), and you'll be able to use it just as you would any other After Dark module. And, yes, you can have the original version of Flying Toasters installed in addition to your custom version.

Once you've gotten the hang of working in ResEdit, you can make more radical alterations to existing modules. Flying irons, anyone?

Boris Speaks In Tongues

You can use ResEdit to alter sound as well as graphics. In this example, we'll alter one of the sound resources in the Boris module. For this example, we'll cannibalize a sound from another After Dark module. After a little practice, you might want to insert your own sounds. You can find sound files online services like CompuServe or America Online. Some

101

user groups offer disks of sounds as well. If you're ambitious, you can create your own custom sounds with MacRecorder, or use the sound recording capabilities that are built into the Macintosh IIsi or LC. *Tip: Make sure the new sound you use is approximately the same size as the sound you're replacing; large sound files may not play correctly.*

1. Make a copy of Boris and a copy of Nocturnes.

2. Open ResEdit, locate the copy of the Nocturnes module, and open it with ResEdit.

3. Double-click the snd icon to open Nocturnes' sound resources.

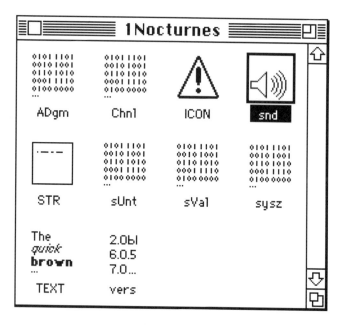

4. When the following window appears, click on the first sound in the list, New Cricket.

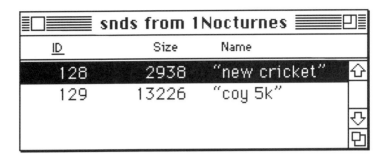

5. Choose Copy from the Edit menu to copy the sound. Then close the snds window and the Nocturnes Copy window.

6. Choose Open from the File menu, and locate and open your copy of Boris.

7. Double-click the snd icon to open Boris' sound resources.

8. Choose Paste from the Edit menu to paste in the cricket sound you just copied. Because the cricket sound has the same ID number as the first Boris sound (ID 128, New Purr), a dialog box will ask you if you want to replace the existing resource 128 with the new one. Click the Yes button. Now, when you look at Boris' sound resources, you'll see that his purr has been replaced by a chirp.

9. Close the snds window, then close the Boris Copy window. When ResEdit asks you if you want to save your changes, click the Yes button.

10. Place your new Boris module in the After Dark Files folder if it's not already there. Rename it if you wish.

Now, when you run the customized Boris module, the cat will behave as he always does until he sits down to purr. At that point, Boris will do a convincing impersonation of a cricket chirping.

To add your own sounds to Boris, copy the sound, repeat the above procedure, and paste the sound into Boris' snds window. You'll need to assign the new sound the same ID number as one of the existing Boris sounds, as follows:

1. In the snds window, click on the sound you want to replace. Jot down the sound's ID number. Let's say, for example, that you want to replace Boris' meow, which is assigned ID 131.

2. Click on the meow sound to select it, then press the Delete button on the Mac's keyboard to delete the meow.

3. Click on the name of your new sound, then select Get Resource Info from ResEdit's Resource menu. You'll see the name and ID number of your new sound. Click on the ID number and change it to 131.

4. Close all open windows in ResEdit, and save your changes.

Now, when you run your copy of Boris, his meow will be replaced by the new sound you inserted.

Custom Eyes-ation

In this example, we'll add a new set of eyes to the Nocturnes module.

1. Make a copy of Nocturnes.

2. Open the copy of Nocturnes with ResEdit. In the window that appears, click the ICON resource icon.

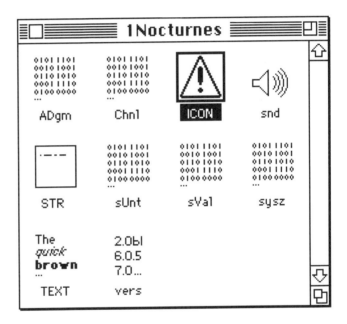

3. The following window will appear:

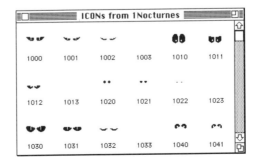

4. Choose Create New Resource from the Resource menu. The ICON ID window will appear.

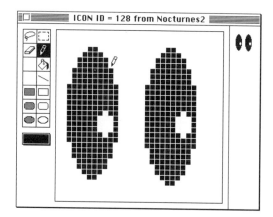

Use ResEdit's drawing tools to create a new pair of eyeballs.

5. When you're satisfied with your new eyes, close the ICON ID window to return to ResEdit's main window. Your new eyes should be selected.

6. Choose Copy, then Paste, from the Edit menu. Click the Unique ID button in the dialog box that appears.

7. Double-click the duplicate eyes and use ResEdit's drawing tools to edit them (in keeping with Nocturnes' format, you should make this pair into phase two of a three-phase blink). Close the ICON ID window and repeat this step for the third set of eyes. Repeat the procedure for the fourth set of eyes, but erase everything in the drawing window this time. Close the ICON ID window.

8. Click on the first set of eyes to select them, then choose Get Resource Info from the Resource menu. Type a new ID number for the first set of eyes (use 1050 for this

example). Do the same for the other three sets, numbering them 1051, 1052, and 1053.

9. Close all ResEdit windows and save your changes.

The next time you activate your custom copy of Nocturnes, a new set of eyes will join the gang. Repeat the steps above to add even more eyes if you wish.

Go ahead and experiment with more modules if you wish. Not all After Dark modules have pictures and sounds you can edit, but you should find enough editable modules to keep you busy for awhile. If you combine your custom modules with other After Dark modules in MultiModule, it's the next best thing to writing your own modules.

Resources

APPLICATIONS

After Dark
Berkeley Systems
2095 Rose St.
Berkeley, CA 94709
510/540-5535

Animation Clips
Media In Motion
P.O. Box 170130
San Francisco, CA 94117
415/621-0707

Capture
Mainstay
5311-B Derry Ave.
Agoura Hills, CA 91301
818/991-6540

Fish! Editor
Tom & Ed's Bogus Software
15600 NE 8th St., Suite A3334
Bellevue, WA 98008

QuickTime Starter Kit
Apple Computer, Inc.
20525 Mariani Ave.
Cupertino, CA 95014
408/996-1010

ResEdit
Apple Programmers and Developers
        Association (APDA)
Apple Computer, Inc.
20525 Mariani Ave, M/S 33G.
Cupertino, CA 95014
800/282-2732

ONLINE SERVICES

America Online
8619 Westwood Center Dr.
Vienna, VA 22182
800/227-6364

CompuServe
P.O. Box 20212
Columbus, OH 43220
614/457-8600, 800/848-8199

USER GROUPS

For information on Mac user groups in your
    area, call Apple at 800/538-9696, ext. 500.

BMUG
1442A Walnut St., Suite 62
Berkeley, CA 94709
510/549-2684

Index

More from Peachpit Press. . .

Canned Art: Clip Art for the Macintosh, 2nd Edition

Erfert Fenton and Christine Morrissett
Voted Best Book of 1990 by *MacWeek*'s Ezra Shapiro, this second edition is an encyclopedia of over 15,000 images, meticulously indexed to help the graphics professional make qualified purchases. A special section covers clip art management, file formats, and printing options, and provides tips on cutting, pasting, and modifying images. The book contains tear-out coupons worth over $1,000 in discounts on clip art packages. *(640 pages)*

Canvas 3.0: The Book

Deke McClelland
Officially endorsed by Deneba Software, publishers of Canvas, this book takes you on a fact-filled tour through the heart and soul of the program. It includes essential information about using Canvas with System 7, creating dynamic illustrations and text effects, and much more. *(384 pages)*

Desktop Publisher's Survival Kit

David Blatner
This book/disk package provides insights into publishing on the Macintosh: troubleshooting print jobs, working with color, scanning, and selecting fonts. The kit also covers everything from graphics file formats and digital fonts to word processing, color, typography, style sheets and printing techniques. A disk containing 12 top desktop publishing utilities, 400K of free clip art, and two fonts is included in this package. *(176 pages)*

Desktop Publishing Secrets

Robert Eckhardt, Bob Weibel and Ted Nace
This compilation offers updated and expanded versions of the 500 best tips and Q&A answers from *Publish* magazine's columns. *The Publish Book of Tips* covers all the major publishing programs on both the PC and Macintosh

platforms and includes *Publish*'s most experienced writers. *(536 pages)*

EcoLinking: Everyone's Guide to Environmental Information

Don Rittner
Eco-activism is just a keystroke away! *EcoLinking*, the first guide to this growing phenomenon, details how computer networks, bulletin boards, and online services can be put to work to save the planet. The book shows how to access the immense environmental information found on worldwide computer networks and explains how to conduct online scientific and environmental research using bibliographic retrieval services, CD-ROM databases, and news services. *(300 pages)*

Illustrator Illuminated

Clay Andres
This book is for people who want to know more about Adobe Illustrator than the manuals can tell them. *Illustrator Illuminated* uses full-color graphics to show how professional artists use Illustrator's tools to create a variety of styles and effects. Each chapter shows the creation of a specific illustration from concept through completion. The book also discusses using Illustrator in conjunction with Adobe Streamline and Adobe Photoshop. *(200 pages)*

The Little Mac Book, 2nd Edition

Robin Williams
Praised by scores of magazines and user group newsletters, this concise, beautifully written book covers the basics of Macintosh operation. It provides useful reference information, including charts of typefaces, special characters, keyboard shortcuts, and a special update on System 7. *(184 pages)*

The Little Mac Word Book

Helmut Kobler

For users new to Microsoft Word or for experienced users who want to familiarize themselves with the features of version 5.0, this book is just the ticket. In addition to discussing Word basics, it provides concise and clear information about formatting text; using Word with Apple's new System 7 operating system; taking advantage of Word's writing tools, including its spelling checker, thesaurus and grammar checker; setting up complex tables, and much more! *(240 pages)*

The Little System 7 Book

Kay Yarborough Nelson

This first-rate reference book explains everything you need to know to take advantage of System 7's virtual memory, desk accessories, and the new Finder and Control Panel. It covers TrueType, tricks for multitasking, and ways to customize your system. *(160 pages)*

The Macintosh Bible, 4th Edition

Sharon Aker (edited by Arthur Naiman)

The best-selling Mac book ever, with over 600,000 copies in print. This book is now revised to include more late-breaking Mac info. Includes free updates. *(1,280 pages)*

The Mac is not a typewriter

Robin Williams

This bestselling, elegant guide to typesetting on the Mac has received rave reviews for its clearly presented information, friendly tone, and easy access. Twenty quick and easy chapters cover what you need to know to make your documents look clean and professional: em dashes, curly quotes, spaces and indents, special characters, hyphenating line breaks, and more. *(72 pages)*

PageMaker 4: An Easy Desk Reference

Robin Williams

Useful for both beginners and advanced users, this book uses a unique, three-column format to answer any PageMaker question as quickly as possible. *(784 pages)*

The QuarkXPress Book, 2nd Edition

David Blatner and Keith Stimely

Peachpit's best-selling, comprehensive guide to QuarkXPress and XTensions, now updated for version 3.1, outlines new features and techniques and also gives a thorough and entertaining introduction to the "wild and weird world of color." *(640 pages)*

QuarkXPress 3.1: Visual QuickStart Guide

Elaine Weinmann

This book takes a visual approach to teaching you the basics of QuarkXPress 3.1. Pictures guide you through the program and text is limited to clear, concise commentary. *(200 pages)*

Real World FreeHand 3

Olav Martin Kvern

The ultimate insider's guide to FreeHand, this authoritative and entertaining book first gives the basics and then concentrates on advanced techniques. The optional disk contains a large stock of PostScript special effects. *(528 pages)*

Order Form

(800) 283-9444 or (510) 548-4393
(510) 548-5991 fax

#	Title	Price	Total
	Art of Darkness (with disk)	19.95	
	Canned Art: Clip Art for the Macintosh	29.95	
	Canvas 3.0: The Book	21.95	
	Desktop Publisher's Survival Kit (with disk)	22.95	
	Desktop Publishing Secrets	27.95	
	EcoLinking	18.95	
	Illustrator Illuminated	24.95	
	The Little Mac Book, 2nd Edition	14.95	
	The Little Mac Word Book	15.95	
	The Little QuicKeys Book	18.95	
	The Little System 7 Book	12.95	
	The Macintosh Bible, 4th Edition (September '92)	32.00	
	The Mac is not a typewriter	9.95	
	PageMaker 4: An Easy Desk Reference (Mac Edition)	29.95	
	The QuarkXPress Book, 2nd Edition	27.95	
	QuarkXPress 3.1: Visual QuickStart Guide	14.95	
	Real World FreeHand	27.95	

Tax of 8.25% applies to California residents only. UPS ground shipping: $4 for first item, $1 each additional. UPS 2nd day air: $7 for first item, $2 each additional. Air mail to Canada: $6 for first item, $4 each additional. Air mail overseas: $14 each item.	Subtotal	
	8.25% Tax (CA only)	
	Shipping	
	TOTAL	

Name	
Company	
Address	
City	State Zip
Phone	Fax
❏ Check enclosed	❏ Visa ❏ MasterCard
Company purchase order #	
Credit card #	Expiration Date

Peachpit Press, Inc. • 2414 Sixth Street • Berkeley, CA • 94710
Your satisfaction is guaranteed or your money will be cheerfully refunded!